# DELIVER!

# DELIVER!

How to Be Fast, Flawless, and Frugal

# JIM CHAMPY

© 2012 by James A. Champy

Publishing as FT Press

Upper Saddle River, New Jersey 07458

FT Press offers excellent discounts on this book when ordered in quantity for bulk purchases or special sales. For more information, please contact U.S. Corporate and Government Sales, 1-800-382-3419, corpsales@pearsontechgroup.com. For sales outside the U.S., please contact International Sales at international@pearson.com.

Printed in the United States of America

ISBN-10: 0-13-231246-8
ISBN-13: 978-0-13-231246-2

This product is printed digitally on demand.

Pearson Education LTD.
Pearson Education Australia PTY, Limited.
Pearson Education Singapore, Pte. Ltd.
Pearson Education Asia, Ltd.
Pearson Education Canada, Ltd.
Pearson Educación de Mexico, S.A. de C.V.
Pearson Education—Japan
Pearson Education Malaysia, Pte. Ltd.

**Vice President, Publisher**
Tim Moore

**Associate Publisher and Director of Marketing**
Amy Neidlinger

**Acquisitions Editor**
Megan Graue

**Editorial Assistant**
Pamela Boland

**Development Editor**
Russ Hall

**Senior Marketing Manager**
Julie Phifer

**Assistant Marketing Manager**
Megan Graue

**Cover Designer**
Alan Clements

**Managing Editor**
Kristy Hart

**Project Editor**
Jovana San Nicolas-Shirley

**Copy Editor**
Apostrophe Editing Services

**Proofreader**
Water Crest Publishing

**Indexer**
Lisa Stumpf

**Senior Compositor**
Gloria Schurick

**Manufacturing Buyer**
Dan Uhrig

*This book is dedicated to my dear friend and colleague, Tom Gerrity, from whom I have learned so much about what's important in life and work.*

# CONTENTS

# ACKNOWLEDGMENTS

As always, my best work is done in association with others.
For this book and the others in this series, my thanks go to
the talented editors at Wordworks, Inc.: Donna Sammons
Carpenter, Maurice Coyle, Ruth Hlavacek, Robert Shayerson,
and Robert W. Stock. I am also grateful to my long-time literary
agent, Helen Rees, and my publicist, Barbara Hendra. I am
deeply appreciative of my publisher, Tim Moore, and all of his
colleagues at Pearson: Amy Neidlinger, Megan Colvin, Julie
Phifer, Sandra Schroeder, Jovana Shirley, Gloria Schurick, Lisa
Stumpf, San Dee Phillips, and Sarah Kearns.

Finally, as always, I am grateful to my wife, Lois, and son,
Adam, for their support and advice when I write. They keep me
focused on the important, the real, and the practical.

# ABOUT THE AUTHOR

**Jim Champy** is one of the leading management and business thinkers of our time. His first best seller, *Reengineering the Corporation*, remains the bible for executing process change. His second book, *Reengineering Management*, another best seller, was recognized by *Business Week* as one of the most important books of its time. Champy's last book is *Reengineering Health Care: A Manifesto for Radically Rethinking Health Care Delivery*.

This book, *DELIVER!*, is a part of a series that examines new business models. The earlier books in the series are *OUTSMART!* and *INSPIRE!*. Champy has filled these books with examples of how companies are outsmarting their competition, engaging customers, and operating in fundamentally new ways.

Champy is also an experienced manager and advisor. He is the Chairman Emeritus of Dell Services Consulting Practice and serves on several private and public sector boards. He speaks and writes with the authority of real business experience and brings pragmatism to the world of business. Champy observes that there is not much new in management, but there is a lot new in business—and a lot to learn from what's new.

WHEN I TITLED THIS BOOK *DELIVER!*, I CHOSE A WORD WITH RICH MEANINGS—BRING FORTH, GIVE BIRTH, SET FREE. JOHN ADAMS MARKED THE DECLARATION OF INDEPENDENCE BY INVENTING AMERICA'S "DAY OF DELIVERANCE" (JULY FOURTH). RECALL THE OLD HIGHWAYMAN'S THREAT ("STAND AND DELIVER!"). PONDER THE MODERN IRONY THAT COMMERCIAL BUILDINGS HAVE BACKDOORS MARKED "DELIVERIES." I WOULD ARGUE THAT THE WORD IS SO POWERFUL THAT IT SHOULD MARK FRONT DOORS ONLY.

CHAPTER 1

## THE HIDDEN PROMISE OF THE EVERYDAY

At first glance, the stories I share between these covers might appear implausible. The organizations I studied all had formidable challenges. Some were being tested by the scope of their own ambitions. Others created their own problems or faced daunting market demands. In each case, they recognized that they would have to undertake a serious reordering of their operations—and they diligently pursued that goal, pushing ever upward and reaching amazing altitudes in their accomplishments. This book honors their leaders and their people. To the best of my ability, it also explains their methods and highlights the lessons to be drawn from them.

I've studied a wide variety of enterprises, from a conglomerate of household brands to the U.S. Navy, and I've learned a lot along the way. These organizations, and others discussed in this book, share an impressive ability to delight their stakeholders by delivering far more value than expected.

In today's challenging economic climate, when funds for major initiatives are scarce, the richest source of advantage may be operations, a treasure hiding in plain view. In the pages ahead, I show how smart leaders have achieved the seemingly impossible, delivering more sales, more earnings, more savings, more quality—the list goes on—by rethinking and retooling the basic, day-to-day activities of their organizations.

*Deliver!* is the third in my ongoing series of briefings on business achievers and the ideas and practices that make them successful in the twenty-first century. The first book, *Outsmart!*, was about strategy; the second, *Inspire!*, focused on marketing. This latest book is especially close to home for me. Operational efficiency was at the heart of the work I wrote with the late and much missed Michael Hammer in 1993 called *Reengineering the Corporation*. It spent 41 weeks on *The New York Times* best-seller list, and its ideas were widely put into practice by such companies as American Standard, Procter & Gamble, and Xerox.

To prepare for writing this volume, and its two predecessors, I looked at hundreds of companies and interviewed dozens of business leaders. I was and remain convinced that great new business and management insights were coming not from academic ivory towers, but from companies themselves. Fresh ideas were fermenting in the heat and sweat of daily, on-the-ground competition.

The pages ahead are filled with such ideas. Interestingly, I found no single formula guaranteeing universal success. What I did find were dozens of ingenious solutions to everyday, every-company problems, solutions enabling organizations to keep delivering more.

I also discovered two characteristics that all the organizations shared. They all started by creating a plan that was rooted in a clear understanding of the management processes required to bring about change. And in executing that plan, they demonstrated a commitment to management basics—steady and persistent focus on goals, discipline, and details. Much of this book is about the grittiness of everyday execution.

I ALSO DISCOVERED TWO CHARACTERISTICS THAT ALL THE ORGANIZATIONS SHARED. THEY ALL STARTED BY CREATING A PLAN THAT WAS ROOTED IN A CLEAR UNDERSTANDING OF THE MANAGEMENT PROCESSES REQUIRED TO BRING ABOUT CHANGE. AND IN EXECUTING THAT PLAN, THEY DEMONSTRATED A COMMITMENT TO MANAGEMENT BASICS—STEADY AND PERSISTENT FOCUS ON GOALS, DISCIPLINE, AND DETAILS. MUCH OF THIS BOOK IS ABOUT THE GRITTINESS OF EVERYDAY EXECUTION.

When we were researching and writing the reengineering book in the late 1990s, the case for business change was strong. The world was in recession, and companies were struggling to compete. They saw reengineering as the answer to many of their challenges. But I can safely say that the case for business change today, given the state of the economy, is even greater.

In that kind of environment, there is unrelenting pressure to cut back on costs and headcounts. The obvious risk is going too far, with inadvertent cuts in capabilities, product quality, and service. That's no way to win new customers or keep old ones. But there is another approach: You can make a committed, intense effort to increase your operational efficiency and deliver. That's what the companies in this book have done, and they have used the savings not simply to maintain their competitive position but to boost it.

Each chapter of this book is devoted to a single and useful idea illustrated by one organization and brings that idea to life. Here's a brief look at what's ahead.

▶ Chapter 2, "Paying for Innovation and Making Innovation
Pay": Martin Franklin, Jarden Corporation's longtime
leader, has built a $4.7 billion kaleidoscope of a
conglomerate—more than 100 old-economy brands
ranging from Crock Pot slow cookers to Bicycle playing
cards to K2 skis. He leaves the running of the businesses
to their individual leaders, but only as long as they keep
delivering better products and services.

Franklin doesn't contribute any cash to support the kind
of R&D the businesses need to meet his demand for
constant innovation. He expects them to do it themselves
with the money they save by continuously improving
their operating efficiencies. At the end of 2007, though,
worried about the possibility of a recession, Franklin took
a hand in things, calling for a major change initiative. He
ordered all Jarden's businesses to plan for a 10 percent
revenue loss in 2008, but to keep cutting their operating
costs as though the economy, and their sales, would hold
up. If business had been normal, they would have had
extra cash on hand. When the recession arrived, they had
months of savings to weather the storm. That's vintage
Martin Franklin.

▶ Chapter 3, "Radically Restructuring to Deliver": The U.S.
Navy was going to be ominously short of seaworthy attack
submarines if Captain Dave Johnson failed to torpedo
expenses. Johnson commanded production of the new
Virginia Class sub, a vitally needed addition to the fleet.
He confronted three minefields—a dizzying delivery
schedule, orders to cut costs by $400 million per sub, and
the likelihood of lethal competition between co-builders

Electric Boat and Newport News, both needing to achieve efficiencies neither had ever achieved before.

Johnson forced all hands to see reality. The choice was sink or swim. A breakthrough change exercise made it possible to improve advanced design during full-scale manufacturing. The plans for the sub were digitized, keeping all parties updated on all revisions. Computerized simulations kept the program moving forward at the most efficient pace—too fast would have triggered a cost over-run. A standard parts catalog was created to save money and reduce confusion for the two builders and their suppliers. It was continuous operational improvement on a giant scale, and it delivered.

▶ Chapter 4, "Doing Better Every Day": Bob Arzbaecher, CEO of the conglomerate Actuant, which produces industrial tools and systems, has quadrupled annual sales to $1.7 billion over the last decade. He's done it by acquiring dozens of companies and making sure they all learn to operate in harmony. Their mandatory tune is called LEAD, and acronym for Lean Enterprise Across Disciplines, and it focuses them on constantly improving their operational efficiency. Arzbaecher relies on another program to get newcomers to adopt LEAD in particular and Actuant in general. It's called AIM, for Acquisition Integration Model, and it successfully addresses the problem at the root of most merger failures—a clash of cultures.

AIM lasts 90 days, during which small, top-level teams from the two companies meet for intense, highly structured sessions. Each session deals with a particular area of the company, from strategy to marketing to information technology. There are regular reports to Actuant's leaders. The most important message AIM delivers, though, is that Actuant doesn't buy companies to close them down or take them apart. The object is to add value to the acquired organization by taking advantage of Actuant's scale and applying the LEAD approach. If the new employees join the continuous-improvement chorus, they and their company will do just fine under the Actuant banner. So far, AIM has been right on target.

▶ Chapter 5, "Getting Back to Focus and Discipline": Doug Conant has presided over one of the most remarkable corporate turnarounds in recent history, the comeback of the Campbell Soup Company. Along the way, he made some tough decisions and took a lot of heat. Early on, he cut the dividend and the stock tanked—but he needed the cash to invest in R&D. He fired 300 of the company's 350 top people—but only after they failed to measure up to a performance standard. He sold a profitable brand at a time when Campbell's needed all the profits it could get—but he was determined to focus all the company's resources on its core business.

Conant's most important decision, though, was the most obvious: He was going to take his time. Getting into trouble had been a long process, he told me, and so would getting out of it. He laid down a 10-year recovery plan, broken into three stages with goals to be reached at each stage. He also recognized that he needed the support of Campbell's 23,000 employees: "We had to win in the workplace so we could ultimately win in the marketplace."

And he was ready to devote whatever personal and corporate resources he could muster to that task. Today, the plan is right on track.

► Chapter 6, "Leveraging Quality": Frank Woods became a California grape grower and then a vintner by chance, but there was nothing accidental about his success in the business. There was no premium California wine at the time, and Woods' Clos du Bois label took over that spot with a mellow, approachable product. He found inexpensive ways to promote the wine, pushing it onto restaurant menus and entering every competition. In his first year, 1975, he sold 3,000 cases, and within a decade that figure was up to 200,000.

From the start, Woods was determined not to allow higher volume to lower the quality of his wine. That, he knew, would require a steady infusion of cash, so he looked everywhere for efficiencies. Where competitors had failed, Woods found ways to use mechanized grape harvesting to achieve major savings to invest in quality product. A high-speed bottling line actually improved quality while raising efficiency. Woods sold Clos du Bois in 1988, but the new owners continue to honor his commitment to quality, supported by ever-greater operational efficiency.

As you will discover, the chapters ahead contain a wealth of detail and lessons. I hope that many of those lessons can bring welcome deliverance from your own business headaches in hard times. After all, this book faces its own challenge—living up to its title. Please turn the page and begin deciding for yourself.

THE NEW MILLENNIUM HAD JUST DAWNED, AND THE BRAVE NEW WORLD OF BUSINESS WAS IN THE FULL FLUSH OF THE INTERNET CRAZE. PROFITS, CASH FLOW, AND EVEN REVENUES HAD BECOME IRRELEVANT; WHAT COUNTED WERE CATCHY NAMES, COOL CONCEPTS, AND OFFICE SUITES FULL OF HIP, YOUNG PEOPLE PLAYING PICKUP BASKETBALL WHEN THEY WEREN'T TOSSING OFF BRILLIANT IDEAS. IN THE FEVERISH NEW ECONOMY, ANY KIND OF BRICK-AND-MORTAR BUSINESS WAS JUST <u>BO</u>-<u>RING</u>— SO 1985.

CHAPTER 2

**PAYING FOR INNOVATION AND MAKING INNOVATION PAY: WOW ON A BUDGET**

Martin Franklin thought otherwise. In the early 1990s, Franklin, the British-born son of a merchant banker and corporate raider Roland Franklin, a close associate of Sir James Goldsmith, bought a small string of eyewear shops. He grew it into a $300 million business and sold it for a $50 million personal profit before he turned 30. In 2000, he had a new idea, what he called an anti-Net concept: Put together a collection of solid Old Economy brands, all of them in niche markets.

You may never have heard of Franklin's company, Jarden Corporation. But in 2008, it cracked the *Fortune 500*, and in 2009, Jarden ranked at number 442 with $5.4 billion in sales. Jarden is composed of more than 100 powerful brands, including Coleman camping equipment, Crock Pot slow cookers, First Alert household alarms, K2 skis, Ball home canning jars, Bee and Bicycle playing cards, Rawlings sporting goods, Mr. Coffee coffeemakers, Oster kitchen appliances, and Sunbeam kitchen appliances. The company is a top supplier to Wal-Mart and the thirteenth largest U.S. importer of shipping containers from China.

Every brand Jarden acquires, Franklin tells me, is the market leader in its own niche—a fact that makes the brands almost unassailable because it would cost a competitor so much to build a significant market share. In some cases, he notes, citing Jarden's Ball brand of home canning jars and equipment, "We are the entire industry, and it's only about $140 million. You'd have to spend an awful lot of money just to get a 10 percent share, and then it's only $15 million, hardly worth the bother." That big-fish-in-a-little-pond strategy was there from the start. "I didn't want to bang heads with P&G," he says.

What keeps Franklin's whole heterogeneous house of cards, including Bee and Bicycle, the leading manufacturer of playing cards, from collapsing is his insistence that each of his businesses continually improve its operational efficiency. "We can't rest on our laurels," he explains. "The quickest way to lose market leadership is to become complacent." Thus, each newly acquired company must start out by paring its costs and discarding underperforming products—and then it must find ways to constantly upgrade its everyday execution.

Jarden has clustered its brands into groups that bolster each other. Consumer Solutions includes most of the brands for household use. The Outdoor Solutions group takes in K2 and Volkl skis, Coleman camping gear, Marmot outdoor wear, and Shakespeare fishing equipment, among other brands. The third major consumer group, Branded Consumables, includes Bee and Bicycle playing cards, Ball jars, and Diamond matches. (Jarden also has a unit called Process Solutions, which has lines of plastic, electronic, and zinc products for industrial use; Jarden furnishes the copper-plated zinc used by the U.S. Mint to stamp out pennies.)

All Jarden's lines are linked in its centralized purchasing plan, taking advantage of the whole company's buying power to drive down the prices it pays for raw materials including glass, copper, steel, and tin. Collectively, Franklin says, the company produces plastic that uses 250 million pounds of resin each year. Size brings other blessings: No company short of Wal-Mart can get better shipping rates. But Franklin won't centralize marketing, product development, or innovation—functions, he says, that must be left to the individual businesses to "keep the DNA of each of these individual brands very much alive. Otherwise they get lost in the wash." And to underwrite that innovation, to provide the cash to nurture that DNA, he looks to the proceeds of each company's ever-improving operational efficiency.

Jarden has developed a powerful business plan: Concentrate on improving the basics—manufacturing, quality control, logistics, packaging—and then feed those savings back into the crucial development processes that will ensure the brands' future. By watching pennies, as it were, the dollars take care of themselves.

**JARDEN HAS DEVELOPED A POWERFUL BUSINESS PLAN: CONCENTRATE ON IMPROVING THE BASICS—MANUFACTURING, QUALITY CONTROL, LOGISTICS, PACKAGING—AND THEN FEED THOSE SAVINGS BACK INTO THE CRUCIAL DEVELOPMENT PROCESSES THAT WILL ENSURE THE BRANDS' FUTURE. BY WATCHING PENNIES, AS IT WERE, THE DOLLARS TAKE CARE OF THEMSELVES.**

Because Jarden's operational approach has such great potential for companies of every size and variety, I have made it the central focus of this chapter. Given the state of the world economy, the resources available for research and development are inevitably going to shrink. You can make up for that shortfall with savings on operations.

# HERE'S HOW JARDEN DELIVERS

In his quest for anti-Net businesses, the first brand to catch Franklin's eye was Ball, the fabled home-canning jar first marketed in 1886. Spun off from the Ball Corporation into a company called Alltrista, the business had been puttering along on its century of momentum. But to Franklin, Ball was a deep-seated consumer brand that still had leverage with nearly every homemaker in the United States. He bought 9.9 percent of Alltrista's stock and offered to buy the whole company. When its directors turned him down, he took a seat on the board and soon persuaded his colleagues to buy into his vision of the brand and make him the CEO. Only 34 years old, he took over in September 2001.

Franklin's first move was to fire 23 staffers and move Alltrista's headquarters from Indianapolis, Indiana, to a modest office park in Rye, 20 miles north of New York City. He believes strongly, he tells me, that "the quality of a business is in inverse proportion to the size of its head office. The smaller the headquarters, the better the company." Even today, with sales well over $5 billion, Jarden's headquarters remains in the same building, with a seasoned executive team there that work closely with the segment leadership who operate each of the business units.

Next, Franklin sold off Alltrista's money-losing plastics business, an ill-judged previous acquisition, to clear up his balance sheet for future purchases. The first of these was a natural extension of home canning, or as Franklin quickly came to call it, food preservation. The company bought a company called Tilia

International that manufactured a vacuum-sealing machine, FoodSaver, to join Ball jars in the home kitchen. That deal, he boasts, doubled Alltrista's earnings per share on the day of closing.

How could the Ball brand itself be strengthened and adapted for the 21st century? When Franklin had asked Alltrista's former CEO how he would innovate the home canning business, "He actually looked at me like I was nuts." But Franklin sat down with his managers and helped them understand that they were in the consumer products business, and innovation was part of their job. That led to easier-to-fill wide-mouth jars and a revolution in packaging: Instead of closed cardboard cases, the jars were sold in shrink-wrapped clear plastic—not only a quantum leap in consumer appeal, but a major cost-saving as well. Alltrista also started marketing some of its jars filled with cookie mix and moved on to jars in kits with instructions for making jams, jellies, pickles, and the like.

That revealed a major operational problem: Ball's sales force wasn't up to its new role. "They were glorified order-takers, because the product had been selling itself," Franklin explains. Sales training in the new products and expanding distribution became the order of the day. "The philosophy was to try new things, to take something that had been looked at one way and look at it in a completely different way," he says. "We did that, and the business is still thriving."

While all that was happening, Franklin was finding other niches to conquer. He sensed that the early years of the decade were a window of opportunity, offering low interest rates and easy credit; sooner or later the window would close, and he wanted to build the foundation of his organization while it was still possible. In short order, Alltrista snapped up Diamond, with its kitchen matches and plastic utensils, and Lehigh Consumer Products, the nation's foremost maker of rope, cord, and kitchen twine. Now Alltrista had annual revenues of $900 million, a profit margin of 17 percent, and a stock price that had jumped eightfold to $20. Franklin wanted a new name to signal the end of Alltrista's way of life. So he coined one himself: Jar, for the original Ball business, and den, the center of a consumer's home and a lair for his hunting band of brands. In 2003, Jarden split its renamed stock and made the *Forbes* list of "The 200 Up and Coming" U.S. companies.

Jarden never stopped looking for businesses to buy, aiming to create a diversified base broad enough to weather any economic climate. The company didn't rely on investment bankers or other corporate scouts for leads; Franklin and Ian G. H. Ashken, vice chairman and chief financial officer, ferreted out prospective deals in the business press and by word of mouth. Here again the key was in the execution: They spent millions on due diligence checking out details, traveling to inspect branch stores and remote factories, even making cost-cutting plans and lists of candidates for firing before closing a deal. "I kissed a lot of frogs," Franklin recalls. And when each deal was done, he sent a "chief transitions officer" to the latest acquisition to carry out the layoffs and start the cost-savings plans.

The next big target of opportunity was American Household—the former Sunbeam company that had fallen into bankruptcy in an accounting fraud during the reign of the notorious "Chainsaw Al" Dunlap. The company was in surprisingly good shape, Franklin says. The three banks that now owned it had effectively repositioned its jumble of brands, which included Coleman, First Alert, Mr. Coffee, and Oster. But the banks disagreed on strategy and wanted to divest. There were other prospective buyers, but none of them wanted the whole operation. Franklin calculated that if they took the risk of buying all of American Household, the banks would be so eager to make a clean exit that they would accept a low offer. And so they did: Jarden got the company for $746 million in 2005, less than half of it in cash—and promptly shuttered its headquarters, for a savings of $25 million a year.

Franklin meant that to be the end of his personal focus on the detailed operations of the new acquisition. He tells each of his new CEOs, "This is your business." Franklin and the leadership team take a hand in setting strategy, but delivering against it is the job of each unit's CEO. He also structures incentives that reward them richly for running their businesses well. But that doesn't mean that he isn't completely dedicated to making the business units deliver. Leaders are held to a calendar of monthly accountability, a routine and mandatory schedule of updates, and progress reports. As opposed to the more traditional quarterly system, it allows for quicker discover of who is executing well and who is falling short.

The first measure is, logically, the financial plan: Each CEO sets his or her own plan, in consultation with Jarden's executive team, and no CEO who fails to beat the plan gets a bonus. "We'll explain," says Franklin, "'Look, either you're going to do this or we're going to come down and do it ourselves.' But if I have to come in and tell them exactly what to do, I know the first thing I have to do is replace the person I'm talking to."

Some CEOs of the acquired companies have been up to the challenge, but in more cases than not, Franklin tells me, "We have brought in fresh blood at the top" or leapfrogged talented managers from below. In the American Household merger, he found his man in Andy Hill, who had been running the Sunbeam division but had been frustrated that top managers wouldn't let him pursue plans to innovate and grow. That appointment has worked out just fine, but Hill's relationship with Franklin got off to a rocky start when Franklin broke his own rules and tried to dictate an operational detail.

A meritocrat, Franklin was offended by the petty bureaucracy of Sunbeam's parking lot, with places assigned according to rank and seniority. He favors no assigned parking places; those who get to work early should have the best spaces. So, on the first day of Hill's regime, "I went in and said, 'Andy, this isn't who we are, and I want it gone. I want it gone before I leave the building.'" That touched off "a real head-butting session," Franklin explains, ending in a compromise: Hill said he had no problem with changing the parking system, but he had a lot of changes to make to set the business right, and he had to time the moves to make them go down as easily as possible with his workforce of 1,000 people. He promised to get all the changes done, including the parking lot, in three months. Franklin agreed, and in due course, the assigned spaces disappeared.

Hill moved quickly to cut overhead at Sunbeam. For years, the company had been suffering financially with huge inventories of outdoor grills that simply weren't moving. The whole line was summarily dropped. Savings from this and other operational efficiencies were invested in innovative products. A team he dubbed New Sources of Growth called for a redesign of the Oster and Mr. Coffee lines, upgrading their image by converting them from white plastic to stainless steel. An ordinary blender was redesigned and packaged with frozen-drink mixers—and an endorsement from Jimmy Buffet—as the $300 Margaritaville, now a $40 million line of its own.

In its innovation, though, Jarden often goes to great lengths to maintain the feel of the original product. The Mr. Coffee redesign was based on a 35-year-old model. A Sunbeam print ad from 1910, showing a princess iron and its stainless-steel storage case, inspired a new version of the case made of translucent plastic, perfect for holding a hot iron right after it's been used, and a combination compact iron and silicone pouch that accomplishes the same feat on the road. There's no point in buying up great old brands, after all, if you're going to throw away all that good will.

At the same time, the company has shown itself capable of quickly seizing a totally new opportunity when it suddenly appears. That happened several years ago when the popularity of poker suddenly spiked after the game became the basis for a cable channel hit show. Jarden had just finished acquiring United States Playing Card, which had produced nothing but cards for 130 years. With Franklin's urging, the company quickly began producing poker chips, and some substantial new income for its new owner.

Despite his overall hands-off management approach, Franklin always reserves the right to step in when he sees operational details going astray, and he did it again when one of Hill's smaller divisions, the First Alert home alarm system, was faltering. Jarden had just bought a new batch of brands for Hill to run, including Bionaire air cleaners and humidifiers and Crock-Pot slow cookers, adding $700 million to annual sales. Understandably, Hill wasn't focusing on the problems at First Alert—humdrum products lacking innovation and an antiquated fire extinguisher plant in Chicago that was burning through money.

When Franklin told Hill that the business was being run badly by its ineffective president, Hill bristled defensively. "Well, we giveth and we taketh away," Franklin said. "We're going to pull First Alert away from American Household." After more argument, Hill eventually agreed. Franklin recruited a new efficiency-and-innovation-minded president (from First Alert's prime rival, Kidde), and the business picked up quickly. It even developed a revolutionary new fire extinguisher, Tundra, in a small, convenient aerosol can, and its Plug-In Carbon Monoxide Alarm was the top seller of 2008 in Amazon.com's home improvement category. The old Chicago plant has been shuttered and sold.

Along with Franklin and CFO Ashken, who have worked together for decades, the triumvirate atop Jarden includes James E. Lillie, president and chief operating officer, who came aboard in 2003. I had a chance to talk to Lillie, who describes the division of responsibility among the three this way: "It is a team, Martin is the architect, Ian is the financier, and I'm the general contractor." As such, it's his job to make sure his subcontractors, the individual businesses, are constantly improving their operational efficiency and executing against their strategy and delivering agreed upon operational and financial results.

He relies on a network of teams drawn primarily from the businesses themselves and focused on individual companywide needs and missions. To make the most of its scale, for example, Jarden has two dozen supply chain "councils," as they're known, that concentrate on various commodities. Each has a corporate-level facilitator but is actually run by executives from businesses with a special interest or expertise in the particular commodity. The corrugated council, for instance, negotiates purchases of corrugated paper for the entire corporation, and the different businesses buy corrugated off that master agreement. A marketing council purchases ad pages and media time. In addition to finding bargain buys, its members exchange tips on how to achieve the best results at the lowest cost.

"We don't try to have a bunch of corporate wonks pretending they know what is best for each one of the individual businesses," Lillie tells me. And there are other advantages to giving the business executives both operating and corporatewide assignments, he says, "It makes their work more interesting and fulfilling, and it gives them a chance to gain experience in other parts of the organization. It also reduces staffing costs."

"WE DON'T TRY TO HAVE A BUNCH OF CORPORATE
WONKS PRETENDING THEY KNOW WHAT IS BEST
FOR EACH ONE OF THE INDIVIDUAL BUSINESSES,"
LILLIE TELLS ME.

As Lillie describes Jarden's 2007 acquisition of K2 Inc., the California-based manufacturer of skis, fishing gear, technical outerwear, and Rawlings baseball gear, it offers further insight into the company's approach to improving operational efficiency. At the time of the buyout, Jarden anticipated $25 to $50 million worth of synergies over the next 24 months. As it worked out, the synergies amounted to $93 million—over just 18 months.

Jarden's councils have a major role in preparing an integration plan for any acquisition, and after the deal has gone through, they work with the newcomer company to ferret out savings. If the newcomer has a huge requirement for corrugated paper, for example, the corrugated council examines how the company has been buying the paper in hopes of finding a better way and applying it to Jarden. "We try to avoid our hubris gene by not thinking that just because we acquired someone we are somehow better and smarter," Lillie explains.

"WE TRY TO AVOID OUR HUBRIS GENE BY NOT
THINKING THAT JUST BECAUSE WE ACQUIRED
SOMEONE WE ARE SOMEHOW BETTER AND
SMARTER," LILLIE EXPLAINS.

The degree to which an acquired company is absorbed into existing Jarden units varies with the acquisition, he says, adding, "There are no absolutes." In the case of K2, its paint ball business and its licensed sports items, which were distributed to the same end user, were brought together with existing Jarden lines in a unit called Jarden Team Sports, based at Rawlings headquarters in St. Louis, Missouri. Redundant warehousing and offices were eliminated. In Europe, distribution centers were integrated into 13 cross-pollinated facilities during the course of 2009.

The existence of two great ski brands, K2 and Volkl, within the K2 product portfolio offered another opportunity for Jarden to cut costs by bringing them under one roof—"Smashing them together," as Lillie puts it. In this case, temptation was resisted. "I could have saved about $10 million that way," he says. "But they serve different skiing customers, pie and park versus alpine, and I might have lost the same amount of money by confusing the marketplace."

K2 brings out a new line of skis each year with substantial improvements over the previous year. I asked Lillie how the company managed its inventory with such a fashion-driven product. "Very robustly," he replied. The line is built to order, with an overhang of 5 percent or so. The rationale is very Jarden: "I'd rather run out and create desire because of a lack of supply than have all my skis be at 50 percent off the subsequent season."

In his pursuit of efficiency, Lillie makes a conscious effort to
keep an eye on the higher-margin businesses. "Sometimes
we give them leeway because they're making their numbers,"
he says, "and I spend more time with the ones who aren't so
healthy. But I also want to make sure nobody is breaking curfew
on the healthy side." In other words, the mandate to achieve
ever-greater operating efficiency applies universally, to every
one of the company's scores of businesses.

The plummeting stock market of 2008 hammered the
company's shares, egged on by a group of Wall Street short
sellers who have never understood Jarden's rationale and see
it as a raggedy collection of no-potential brands. From a peak
of $44 a share in 2007, the stock had dropped to the $10 level
early in 2009, but by fall was back up to nearly $30. But Franklin
was unperturbed. "That's got nothing to do with our business,"
he tells me matter-of-factly. "Shorts in this environment can
say anything they want. There's not really much I can do about
that."

Jarden prepared early for a serious downturn. In December
2008, the company cut staff across the board by 6 percent,
froze salaries and hiring, and suspended 401(K) payments.
Its businesses were told to plan for 10 percent less revenue—
but they were ordered to cut their costs as though they were
actually going to hit their original revenue budget. If the
economy held up, they would be way ahead of the game. But if
the economy tanked midyear, they would have the benefit of
a full year of savings, and they wouldn't be caught with excess
cash and inventory.

"We are cutting back on all kinds of things," Franklin acknowledges, "Jim has a mantra, prepare for the worst and hope for the best, but I am not cutting back on innovation, and I'm not cutting back on marketing. Those are the engines that drive the business." He's taking a long view of the current recession. Hard times give market leaders an opportunity to grab a bigger share of market, he explains, and "our businesses are gaining market share left, right, and center." And Franklin sees another edge for Jarden in this downturn: As big retailers get a larger share of the nation's buying dollars, "They'll want to deal with larger and more sophisticated vendors." Before Jarden came along, there were no large vendors in niche categories.

The global financial crisis having shut down the credit markets; Jarden is focused on the brands already in its corral; and Martin Franklin sees no need for more any time soon. He's clearly in for the long haul and fit for it: Now 43, he's a regular competitor in Hawaii's Ironman triathlon and the even more grueling Badwater Ultramarathon, billed as the world's toughest footrace across 135 miles of Death Valley desert and mountain terrain. At Jarden, he figures the team has the next several years to cull the herd, fine-tune the businesses, and continue streamlining and growing them with innovations. And when that's done, he says, "I'm hoping that people will look at Jarden exactly the way they see Procter & Gamble or Clorox."

I'd say that's a good bet.

# STAND AND DELIVER

▶ *Forget the status quo.* It's the enemy. If you're not moving ahead, if you're not constantly adjusting to your markets and your competitors and boosting your performance, you're falling behind. That's true for every area of your organization—especially operations. At a time when profits are under extreme pressure, improvements in operational efficiency can provide rare, much-needed funds to support innovation. Because it follows that regimen, Jarden is better equipped to ride out the current economic storm.

▶ *Keep an eye on your high performers.* Just because a business is producing impressive margins is no reason to give it a pass. High profits can mask gross inefficiencies and wasted resources, a good hunting ground for achieving operational efficiency. Until recently, for example, the profits flowed so easily for most pharmaceutical companies that they spent money with little or no discipline with respect to expected returns. Now, with the economy sluggish and Washington determined to cut healthcare costs, these companies are managing their spending much more carefully.

I'm reminded of the old adage that "too much money makes you dumb." Jarden knows better, applying the same rules of efficiency to all of its units, regardless of their margins. Operational efficiency should be an equal opportunity experience.

▶ *Keep tabs.* Unless you constantly monitor your operations, you can't spot weakness and boost efficiency. For the most part, Martin Franklin leaves execution of his strategic decisions to the top executives of his many companies, but he has also established trigger points that alert him when the execution falters. Output is one obvious trigger point: Steady-state or reduced production levels signal a problem. Poor financial results is another: Are costs coming down, and if not, why not?

Note that Jarden requires the heads of its businesses to make formal, detailed presentations on a monthly basis to the executive the executive team. He doesn't believe the standard quarterly reporting model allows him to spot problems in time to take action to keep them from getting serious. When the reporting process showed that the First Alert fire extinguisher plant in Chicago was starting to lose money, for example, a new president was brought in post haste to move operations in the right direction. By demanding the more frequent presentations, Jarden's senior team keeps the leaders of the businesses focused on their mutually established goals.

Technology has transformed our capacity for keeping tabs on operations. But managers still need to engage with each other, on a regular basis, to understand what is really going on.

▶ *Find hidden value in your products.* Jarden does an exceptional job at making its operations more efficient and putting the dollars saved into innovation. But innovation is much more than simply introducing an entirely new product. Sometimes you can deliver more value by repurposing the products you already have or changing the frame of reference of your business. What Jarden did with Ball is an example of both.

Jarden took the humble canning jar and elevated it to a drinking vessel that now shows up in hip bars and restaurants. It filled some jars with cookie mix, and it combined others in kits to make jams and pickles. Jarden saw the hidden value in the product and brand and leveraged that value in whatever way it could.

The company accomplished this by changing its frame of reference for Ball's business. It expanded its offerings by thinking of itself as a consumer products company in the food preservations business, not just in the home canning business. This is more than a choice of words. See if you can find more value in your products by thinking differently about your company and expanding how your products are used.

▶ *Prepare people for what's to come.* Any program to alter your operations is going to create a problematic response, large or small, among your veteran employees. They've likely been operating in a particular way for years, and most any change is going to be unsettling and unwelcome. So it becomes incumbent on you to prepare them for what's coming and to provide incentives and encouragement that assure their cooperation. Preparation is especially important if you follow Jarden's focused, performance-oriented management style.

Explain to employees what you plan and why. Solicit their suggestions, take their ideas seriously, and celebrate those you adopt. Make it clear that the changes will improve profitability and assure the company's future at an economic moment when, as Franklin puts it, no company can afford to rest on its laurels.

▶ *Bring the best forward.* There are all sorts of formalized techniques for identifying future leaders. Many companies maintain lists of their people with high potential and create programs for their development. But nothing better informs management as to an individual's worth than his or her performance on a working team. Jarden's councils provide that opportunity. At the same time, they give the individual a chance to get better acquainted with different aspects of the company as a whole. Your operation may not lend itself to the council approach, but the theory still holds: Look for ways in which managers can, in person, work on projects with the brightest operating people. In addition to preparing for the company's future, you're likely to hear some ideas and insights you would never encounter in your normal, day-to-day rounds.

▶ *Keep corporate thin.* As they grow, many companies build huge corporate staffs along the way. These staffs take on a life of their own, creating unnecessary work for business units, usually in the form of unproductive reporting and control requirements. I have heard many operating executives complain bitterly about the demands of corporate, which they often experience as a distraction from running their business.

Jarden avoids this problem by keeping the corporate staff lean. He also carefully balances the decisions that are made at the top and those that are made below. Strategic decisions, such as what new businesses to enter or what companies to acquire, happen at the corporate level, while the individual business units take care of operating decisions. Only when a business unit gets in trouble, does Franklin intrude. The balancing act is important: If you want to hold your operating people accountable for their performance, you have to let them perform.

▶ *Don't let your size go to waste.* There's no point in building a big organization if you don't leverage that scale to achieve greater operating efficiency, delivering more value with less an investment. Jarden does it by centralizing some key purchasing and service activities. At the same time, the company wisely avoids the temptation to centralize functions like marketing, product development, and innovation that are essential to a business unit's operations. If you call all the shots, your business units are never going to surprise you with great new products and services.

▶ *Sometimes you have to change horses.* When a company begins to expand its product portfolio or begins to add services along with its products, it places major new demands on its people. That happened at Jarden when the team transformed Ball from a manufacturer of empty canning jars to a real consumer products brand. Suddenly, the sales force was given a whole new mandate that called for skills it lacked. Computer hardware companies encountered the same problem when they began selling services along with their hardware.

It takes more sophistication to sell a service than a jar or a box. So if that's your plan, you have to pave the way by making sure your people can handle the change. A change in skills—or a change in personnel—may be required.

IN THE FALL OF 2005, THE U.S. NAVY'S
SUBMARINE PROGRAM WAS FOUNDERING.
THE HEYDAY OF THE LOS ANGELES CLASS
NUCLEAR-POWERED, FAST-ATTACK SUB, THE
BACKBONE OF THE FLEET AND ONE OF THE
STARS OF TOM CLANCY'S NOVEL *THE HUNT
FOR RED OCTOBER*, WAS LONG PAST. ITS
REPLACEMENT, THE SEAWOLF CLASS, WAS
SCUTTLED AFTER PENTAGON POLICYMAKERS
DEEMED IT OUTMODED AND FAR TOO COSTLY
IN A WORLD WHERE THE COLD WAR NO
LONGER RAGED. AND NOW CONSTRUCTION
DELAYS AND COST OVERRUNS THREATENED
THE NEW VIRGINIA CLASS AS WELL. WITHOUT
FAST ACTION, AMERICA WOULD FIND HERSELF
PERILOUSLY SHORT OF ATTACK SUBMARINES.

CHAPTER 3

RADICALLY RESTRUCTURING TO
DELIVER: TAKE HER DOWN A
HALF BILLION

Admiral Michael G. Mullen, who was then Chief of Naval Operations and is now Chairman of the Joint Chiefs of Staff, decided to shake up the troops. Attending the annual submarine conference of the National Defense Industry Association in September, he took to the podium to order the doubling of Virginia's one-per-year production rate, starting in 2012. But there was one huge caveat: The Navy would pay no more than $2 billion each for the subs. Period. Executives for the two companies responsible for building the vessels were aghast. How would they slash $400 million off the cost of each submarine? Even more difficult, how would they do so while the ship was already in production?

The military-industrial complex is among the least likely places you might expect to find an example of ambitious, rigorous, and efficient cost-cutting. To many, defense contracting is the embodiment of bureaucracy, waste, and profiteering. But the U.S. Navy and its two shipbuilder partners in the Virginia class program have an entirely different—and inspiring—story to tell. Theirs is a tale of excellence in process design and everyday execution on a massive scale and more than a decade of nonstop effort.

They didn't have the option of incremental change; this was not the kind of crisis that would be solved by changing a process or two. As major companies and industries have found to their dismay, when a product needs to be redesigned, its manufacture often has to be rethought as well. And in this case, the redesign and the new manufacturing process had to be done on-the-fly, with the program already under way. Survival required the transformation of the basic business model.

**THEY DIDN'T HAVE THE OPTION OF INCREMENTAL CHANGE; THIS WAS NOT THE KIND OF CRISIS THAT WOULD BE SOLVED BY CHANGING A PROCESS OR TWO.**

The Navy's Virginia class program, which continues to this day, has turned a looming disaster into a cost-cutting victory. It is reengineering on steroids, an achievement that holds important lessons for people in both the private and public sectors.

Beyond that, the program is a significant and surprising new variation on an old technique, continuous improvement. Continuous improvement takes as its starting point a fixed product design. Then the focus shifts to a never-ending effort to reduce labor and manufacturing costs. That line of attack wouldn't yield much benefit for the Virginia class, though, with labor and manufacturing comprising only one-third of the submarine's total cost. So instead, the Navy and the two shipbuilders took continuous improvement to the next level, applying it across the board. Every detail of the operation, from the initial design to the final adjustments before delivery, would be scrutinized. In theory, the $2 billion target price would be reached progressively as continuous revisions in the total program whittled away costs. It was time to deliver.

# A DEEPER DIVE

The story of the Virginia really begins in 1976 when the first Los Angeles class attack sub slid down the ways. It was fast, quiet, and capable of missions ranging from sinking surface ships and battling enemy subs to launching missiles at onshore targets. All told, 62 were built, each with a life expectancy of 33 years. A bigger, faster, better-armed, and even quieter submarine, the Seawolf class, was supposed to replace the Los Angeles subs, but the Seawolf was extremely expensive (up to $3.2 billion each) and meant mainly for deepwater use. The end of the Cold War brought a need for more flexible, shallow-water operations at a more reasonable cost, so Seawolf construction was canceled after only three ships were completed, and the Virginia class subs were designed. In 1995, the Navy committed to building 30 of them at a planned cost of $2.2 billion each.

Problems surfaced from the beginning. Four subs were ordered as the first stage of the program. By 2005, 10 years into the project, only one ship had been delivered, and three were still under construction. But costs were running fully 41 percent over the 1995 estimates. Under Congressional rules, that triggered a review.

From an operations point of view, the cost overruns weren't surprising. Unlike big guns, say, or fighter-bombers, new warships are built without prototypes; the first one built *is* the prototype. That the first ship of the class, *USS Virginia*, was delivered within 2 months of a target set fully a decade earlier was a vindication of sorts for the program. But the cost overruns couldn't be tolerated, and the review was followed by an order to cut $5 billion from the budget and slow down the schedule. In the second stage of the program, six subs were to have been built at a pace of two per year. But after the review, deliveries were pared to just one annually.

Paradoxically, the delay put the program in even greater peril. The slower the pace of building, the harder it became to hold down costs. In part, this was just inflation at work: A ship delivered in 2020 would inevitably cost more than one built a decade earlier. But costs also rose because the builders and their subcontractors had to carry their overhead expenses over the longer span of the contract and couldn't order supplies quickly enough to get full advantages of scale. The stretched-out schedule was going to add $200 million to the cost of each ship, raising the price to $2.4 billion even if the earlier cost overruns were eliminated. And to hit Mullen's $2 billion target, each new submarine would have to cost fully $860 million less than *USS Virginia* and *USS Texas*, the first two ships in the class.

One of the biggest problems, however, was just the formidable and growing complexity of a nuclear submarine. Each Virginia class ship contains more than 1 million components, which is 10 times the number of parts in a 777 jetliner, all of which must work under extreme conditions. The standard sonar system, for instance, required that 1,000 holes be drilled through the submarine's hull, each of which had to be sealed and tested to withstand the colossal water pressure at a depth of 800 feet— that's 347 pounds per square inch, or nearly 50,000 pounds per square foot. The Los Angeles class subs had each taken 6 to 7 million worker-hours to build. The *Virginia* ate up more than twice as much: 14.6 million worker-hours.

EACH VIRGINIA CLASS SHIP CONTAINS MORE THAN 1 MILLION COMPONENTS, WHICH IS 10 TIMES THE NUMBER OF PARTS IN A 777 JETLINER, ALL OF WHICH MUST WORK UNDER EXTREME CONDITIONS.

Complicating the problems, the contractors were working under several serious constraints. The cancellation of the Seawolf program had meant a 4-year gap in submarine production. During that time the nation's primary submarine builder, General Dynamics's Electric Boat shipyard in Groton, Connecticut, had to lay off nearly one-third of its workforce of 15,000. The second prime contractor, the Northrop-Grumman shipyard at Newport News, Virginia, hadn't built a submarine in a decade. Newport News, too, had lost skilled workers. And the shipbuilders' network of 12,000 suppliers had thinned considerably during the lull in submarine orders; 80 percent of them were now the sole sources of their components, so there was less competition to keep prices in check.

The Navy's concerns went beyond the price tag. To meet its readiness standards, the service required a minimum of 48 attack submarines. Given the inexorable retirement schedule of Los Angeles class subs, building just one new ship per year would soon pare the fleet to only 33. If the pace could be stepped up to two ships a year by 2012, however, the number of subs would drop at the low point to just 41 before rising again to 48.

Those were the considerations that led Admiral Mullen to issue his cost-cutting challenge as a condition for the two-a-year production rate. His next task: Find the right officer to run the program. Captain Dave Johnson was chosen to walk this particular plank.

# CHARTING A NEW COURSE

Johnson had been working on the construction and
maintenance of submarines almost from the day he graduated
from the Naval Academy in 1982. After a stop at my alma mater,
the Massachusetts Institute of Technology, for an advanced
degree, he had helped build the Seawolf class and had a hand in
the design of the Virginia class subs.

His first order of business, Johnson tells me, was to encourage
teamwork between the two builders, notwithstanding their
longstanding fierce rivalry in building the Los Angeles and
Seawolf submarines. Technically, Electric Boat was the prime
contractor, with Newport News as the lead subcontractor. That
relationship worked out, Johnson says, because "The fee was
split equally between the two teammates. You were naturally
incentivized to help each other, because you both got hurt on
the fee if the other guy overran."

The contract itself was ingeniously structured to encourage
cost-cutting and continuous improvement. The first four ships
were to be built under a conventional cost-plus-fixed-fee
deal, but the next six promised a fixed price for each ship with
$231 million of profits tied to five specific incentives: labor
cost control, material cost control, schedule performance
on benchmark events, total cost performance, and capital
expenditures that would reduce costs. That last clause was
especially clever: After one of the companies proposed a capital
expenditure plan and the Navy approved it, the Navy would
pay half the cost of the capital improvement up front. The
second half would be paid only after the savings were actually

booked—and if those savings didn't materialize, the Navy would take back its payment for the first half.

Teamwork also depended heavily on the program managers for the two shipbuilders, John Holmander at Electric Boat and Becky Stuart at Newport News. In the beginning, Holmander tells me, his people saw collaboration as "an unnatural act—here you are linking up and lashing up with your competitor." But it worked, and in his view—whatever Johnson's theories about the incentive of shared profits—the motivating factor was pride in the job and a sense of mission in building submarines. "We had a will to make it work," Holmander says. "We have truly come up with a common goal, and working together we have built trust. When it comes to getting the job accomplished and building submarines at an affordable price with high quality, we all share that culture; we all share that desire for goodness."

WE HAD A WILL TO MAKE IT WORK," HOLMANDER SAYS. "WE HAVE TRULY COME UP WITH A COMMON GOAL, AND WORKING TOGETHER WE HAVE BUILT TRUST. WHEN IT COMES TO GETTING THE JOB ACCOMPLISHED AND BUILDING SUBMARINES AT AN AFFORDABLE PRICE WITH HIGH QUALITY, WE ALL SHARE THAT CULTURE; WE ALL SHARE THAT DESIRE FOR GOODNESS."

"We worked very hard on having a good working and communication relationship," Johnson notes. The value of that relationship became evident early in the program when

Newport News, building *USS Texas*, its first submarine in a decade, ran into trouble coordinating the job.

Under the contract, systems for each ship—the drinking water system, say, or the system of trim tabs, pumps, and drains that keeps the sub level in the water—were treated as units and turned over to the Navy after inspection and testing. As Johnson paraphrased the handoff, "Okay, ship force guy, now you own it." But the sophisticated metrics that Johnson had set up showed that delays in these turnovers were threatening *Texas*'s planned 84-month construction schedule. The Navy had to tell both builders to stop work on some parts of the ship until the whole job got back on track—a delay that stretched the building of *Texas* to 94 months, but held its cost even with *Virginia*'s at $2.86 billion.

"Without that kind of sharing the details between the senior levels at the companies and me," Johnson says, "we could have actually run out of money before the ship went to sea." As it turned out, *Texas* did go to sea, on its initial trials, in May 2006.

In one way, Mullen's challenge gave the shipbuilders a kind of head start on meeting the target: Half of the $400 million cost-saving per ship would be achieved automatically by doubling the building pace to two subs a year, thus halving the overhead time and mitigating the effects of inflation. But the other $200 million would be a good deal harder, and it had to be firmly in prospect before the schedule could speed up.

The Virginia class was designed using integrated process and product design (IPPD) principles. Johnson offered this translation: "We designed it based on how we were going to build it." The ship's thick steel pressure hull, for example, was to be built in sections, or modules. Each module would be fitted out with as many of its interior furnishings as possible in the factory, before being welded together, so that large, complex engines, weapons systems and the like wouldn't have to be taken apart, carried in through the hatch and reassembled in the tight confines of the finished hull. This mandate reflected the "1 - 3 - 8" rule, that a job that takes 1 hour in the shop will take 3 hours in a factory setting or fully 8 hours of work in the pressure hull.

And the design could be changed to accommodate the construction process: Bulky components, for instance, were repositioned so they didn't sit where two hull sections joined and could thus be installed as the module was being built. That move alone saved $1 million and five weeks in building time.

The design itself had been digitized, so that everyone involved could call up any detail with its latest revisions. *Virginia* was the first ship ever built to a digital design, according to Holmander, and the first to use IPPD, which helped cement the unlikely new culture of teamwork. The constant consultation and visualizing of potential problems let everyone see everyone else's point of view, he said, so Electric Boat's operations and engineering people "were learning how to get along better than they had ever gotten along before." That, in turn, eased relations with the former foes from Newport News.

Perhaps the most revolutionary improvement was the Navy's decision to spend $600 million after production had begun to look back and revise the basic design in light of the production experience. That expense was worthwhile because, as a RAND Corporation study had shown, much bigger savings are possible in the design and production planning stages than in actual production. Among other major improvements, the look back resulted in a huge increase in the size of each hull module. The 377-foot-long *Virginia* and *Texas* were built in 10 sections each. The modules grew and their numbers shrank until *New Hampshire*, the fifth ship in the program, was built in just four sections, each crammed with preinstalled equipment that didn't have to be wrestled into a closed hull. All told, Johnson says, the $600 million investment in improving planning saved the Navy about $1.4 billion over the first two stages of the program.

Electric Boat and Newport News both built modules, with the work assigned to fit each yard's capabilities. Electric Boat, for instance, had specialized equipment for turning out cylindrical sections of pressure hull, and thus was assigned the modules in the middle of each sub. Newport News got the tricky job of machining the domed ends of the pressure hull.

Final assembly of the submarines alternated between the two companies, and as the modules grew, transporting them between the shipyards became a bigger challenge. Holmander was in charge of that. He found huge 78-wheel transporters that could be linked together to move a hull module weighing 2,000 tons. Electric Boat already had a barge big enough for the job, but Holmander added some safety features and stabilizing gear. Then he built a machine that literally lifted the barge out of the water on three huge jacks to the level of the pier, so the transporters with their 2,000-ton burden could be rolled on and off the barge.

All told, Holmander had to invest $13 million in the system— but it saved 1.2 million man-hours of labor per ship. It took 8 hours to float a module from Electric Boat's manufacturing plant in Quonset Point, Rhode Island, to its assembly plant in Groton, Connecticut. The journey to or from Newport News took 48 hours, and Holmander paid a lot of attention to the weather forecasts.

Not incidentally, the continual design improvements were upgrading the ships even as they saved production dollars. The sonar system, for example, was redesigned to reduce its size, eliminate all those hull penetrations, and use hydrophones good for the life of the ship instead of much costlier transducers that last only half as long. The changes increased the sub's payload volume by 50 percent, to 2,100 cubic feet, while saving $11.1 million per submarine.

Electronic systems were redesigned to come in standard-size packages that fit into a central rack, so "It's not a big deal," Johnson explains, to update a system when technology evolves. And a seemingly simple innovation, the large aperture bow array, enables a Virginia class sub to make major changes in its payload as its mission changes.

Traditional submarines have few openings to the outside world, and those few are understandably small. But that severely limits what subs can carry. Anything that won't go down the hatch must enter or exit through a sub's torpedo tubes. And as

Johnson observes, "A lot of the griping about the submarine force is that everything has been constrained to a 21-inch-wide hole." The wide aperture array offers bigger holes, clustering the sub's 12 Tomahawk missile launchers into two bundles in the bow of the ship, each 87 inches in diameter. Removing one cluster enables the sub to load objects more than 7 feet wide, and also permits for replacing the missiles with other cargo—multiple torpedoes, a small robot submarine, or even a team of 11 Navy SEALs with all their equipment. The sub also has a tank that functions as a lock to pass divers in and out of the ship, and it has special depth-controlling gear to keep it hovering steadily while the SEALs are at work.

Production planning and the actual building processes were monitored just as carefully as the design. Computer-based simulations of various manufacturing and scheduling scenarios kept the program on track, accurately predicting how a planned change would affect the schedule and how each change would raise or lower total costs. One such study, for example, showed that trying to push production too fast would actually increase costs, pointing the way to the most efficient overall pace.

All the while, the two shipyards were building their own cost-cutting facilities under the Navy's capital expenditure program. The biggest of these projects was Holmander's $13.1 million barge upgrade; the next was Electric Boat's plant for coating each hull section with two inches of rubber—a feature whose function Johnson leaves determinedly vague, "I'll just say there's a two-inch-thick rubber coat on the ship." At first, the rubber was applied in dry dock after the submarine was assembled and delivered. By coating individual modules and touching up the joints during assembly, the $9.4 million invested in the coating facility will save $71 million over the life of the program. Even better, it will speed up the delivery of each submarine by 6 to 9 months. The more than 150 capital expenditure projects have saved $150 million per ship and will trim $3 billion over the life of the program. The return on the Navy's investment has been more than 7-to-1, a win in anyone's book.

Continuous improvement was more than a slogan. With Holmander and Becky Stuart, Johnson found efficiencies and savings at every stage of building the ships. "We're constantly evaluating the way we perform the work," says Holmander. "We have a joint corrective action board for quality improvements. And whenever we deliver a ship, we also have what we call a hot wash. We'll bring the people from Electric Boat, Newport News, and the Navy together, and we'll do a critical appraisal of all of our work and put together an action agenda" to correct any problems turned up in the wash.

In the radio room, for instance, refinements in development, installation, and testing produced savings of more than $20 million; just-in-time delivery cut another $15 million from the cost of electronic systems. Each completed hull module became the benchmark to beat for its counterpart on the next ship. The shipyards, Johnson says, were constantly "challenged to beat the best they've ever done on every module. They just have a continuous improvement mindset."

# FULL THROTTLE

By the time Mullen issued his challenge in 2005, great progress
had already been made in cutting the costs of the program.
The first ship, *Virginia*, had cost $2.86 billion, and *Texas*, still
in the yard, would cost the same. But the builders had learned
enough to know that they could save more than 2 million
worker-hours and $330 million on the next two ships, *Hawaii*
and *North Carolina*, which were well along when Mullen spoke;
and they expected *New Hampshire*, which had been started in
2002, to come in at $2.4 billion. So they had already cut costs by
nearly $500 million per ship, and Mullen took that into account
in setting his target of $2 billion per ship in 2005 dollars. But
now it was time to sail into uncharted water. With half the
remaining $400 million to be saved just by doubling the pace of
construction, how could the builders find the last $200 million
in savings?

The answer, in effect, was by doing more of the same.
Continuous improvement went right on happening, with one
refinement after another. Individually, the savings got smaller,
but they all added up. Streamlining the process of shock-
testing the ship to ensure that it could withstand near-misses in
combat saved another $72 million per ship; at last count, more
than 100 process improvements had cut costs by $61 million.
Now the focus was on shortening the total construction time
for each sub, which would reduce worker-hours, save more
overhead, and speed up deliveries.

Holmander started a standard parts catalog, trying to specify common components that the two shipyards and their suppliers could use to save costs. He also leaned on suppliers to cut their costs and the time they took to deliver components. The subs' main engines, for instance, were being manufactured by Northrop Grumman Marine Systems in California, and they were taking 48 months to make. On his first visit to the plant, Hollander suggested that 32 months would be better. "I didn't get a 'Hell, no,'" he recalled. "To me, that was a good sign that they were willing to work with us; and they have." Both the production time and the price of the engines turned out to be negotiable.

When a production bottleneck developed because of delays in delivery of a classified component that Holmander identifies only as "acoustic damping material," he visited the tiny plant that produces the stuff and worked out a solution. But he was bothered that the whole program depended on this three-person operation and its unique, proprietary product, so he asked the Navy's research scientists to develop an equivalent material—which they did, to be produced in case of an emergency with the contractor. "So we fixed the problem," Holmander says, "but we also de-risked it."

All these efforts slowly whittled the time needed to build submarines. The original budget called for 84 months to construct each ship. *New Hampshire* would take only 71 months, and the tenth ship, *Minnesota*, would be built in 64 months. The goal now is to produce the third block of 20 ships in 60 months each.

Until 2007, the builders lacked a simple way to keep track of the cost reductions as they phased in and continuously lowered the total cost. It was Navy Secretary Donald C. Winter who suggested that the program could use a metric similar to the aircraft industry's burn-off chart, which tracks weight reductions in planes under development. This became the Virginia Class Glide Slope, a chart with a target line slanting down from $2.2 billion in August 2005, to $2 billion in March 2008, and another bumpier line showing the actual progress as one saving after another kicked in.

Early in 2009, the bumpy line reached the $2 billion mark. There was jubilation in two shipyards, applause in Congress, and quiet satisfaction in the Defense Department. The savings were so real and tangible that Dave Johnson could hand back $48 million in Navy funding for the fiscal year. The Virginia class program was given its third David Packard Excellence in Acquisition Award, and Johnson got a promotion to Vice Admiral for leading it. But the real prize was handed down when the Navy agreed to accelerate the program to two ships per year, starting not in 2012, the original goal, but a full year earlier.

All told, the Navy's Virginia class submarine program has been an epic—innovative continuous improvement on a vast scale, over a decade of constant vigilance and teamwork by three giant organizations. The Navy found ingenious ways to motivate its contractors to keep costs down, and the managers' focus on that job never flagged. It's a truly remarkable story, and it raises an interesting question: If they could deliver, why can't we all?

ALL TOLD, THE NAVY'S VIRGINIA CLASS
SUBMARINE PROGRAM HAS BEEN AN EPIC—
INNOVATIVE CONTINUOUS IMPROVEMENT ON
A VAST SCALE, OVER A DECADE OF CONSTANT
VIGILANCE AND TEAMWORK BY THREE GIANT
ORGANIZATIONS. THE NAVY FOUND INGENIOUS
WAYS TO MOTIVATE ITS CONTRACTORS TO
KEEP COSTS DOWN, AND THE MANAGERS'
FOCUS ON THAT JOB NEVER FLAGGED. IT'S A
TRULY REMARKABLE STORY, AND IT RAISES AN
INTERESTING QUESTION: IF THEY COULD DELIVER,
WHY CAN'T WE ALL?

# STAND AND DELIVER

> ▶ *Demolish the stove pipes.* I learned in my reengineering
> days that people who work in different business functions
> develop different points of view. Although designers strive
> for a product that satisfies their customers' needs, they
> may pay little attention to how it will be built. Managers in
> manufacturing make a product to conform to a design but
> are unlikely to look for ways that it might be redesigned for
> easier production. Business leaders have long sought to
> bridge the chasm between design and manufacturing, yet
> it remains a fact of corporate life.

When the Virginia class was in the planning stage, the
Navy was determined to avoid that hazard. As Dave
Johnson says, "We designed it based on how we were
going to build it." The design of the sub was developed
along with the methods to be used to manufacture it, and

both the design and the processes were modified to get the best overall result. And because the work was done digitally, it could be easily shared, and commented upon, by all involved.

Not all businesses are an ideal venue for Integrated Process and Product Design (IPPD) in its true form, which relies on a so-called Integrated Product Team (IPT) devoted to the merging of design and production into a single, comprehensive plan. But the principle holds: Much stress and much error can be avoided by demanding collaboration between the people who design the product and those who manufacture it.

▶ *Big moves call for big change.* As a proponent of the more radical reengineering approach to change, I have often had my doubts about continuous change programs. That's mostly because continuous change is usually associated with incrementalism: Just keep changing a little bit regularly, and you will eventually reach your goal.

But when major change is required in both product and process—as was the case in the Virginia sub program—incrementalism alone won't cut it. The unique quality of what the Navy did here was to focus continually on changes that were big. It's an approach that requires a real appetite for change and a great ambition.

▶ *Think mission impossible (almost).* When I first heard the story of the Virginia sub program, I was incredulous. How could two highly competitive companies join forces to build an enormously complex warship and actually succeed by doing so in a shorter time and at a lower cost? That's hard enough when there's only one company involved. The answer, it turned out, includes all sorts of smart moves on the part of the Navy and the companies, but what makes it all work is the high sense of mission this team shares. It's not just about building a great boat and meeting a daunting technical challenge—which alone are inspiring. It's also about the compelling security needs of their country in a new geo-political environment. The overriding mission here is to do whatever must be done to protect the nation. In the eyes of this team, failure is not an option.

Every enterprise of any value should have a clear and clearly communicated mission that inspires a shared commitment. Does your company mission measure up to that standard?

▶ *Look upstream.* It's no secret in the engineering and manufacturing world that early design decisions determine most of a product's cost. When a design is locked in, any major changes are prohibitively expensive. During the Virginia sub program, the Navy avoided the need for big changes by continuously "looking upstream." It kept studying how components were placed in the sub's sections, for example, and making design changes to improve the positioning of bulky components in the hull. Such changes produced substantial savings and improved the sub's performance.

If you are in business-to-business relationships, selling materials or components to customers that incorporate your product into theirs, understanding and influencing your customers' design process could save lots of costs, for all parties. Keep looking upstream, questioning your—and sometimes your customer's—design decisions.

▶ *Practice transparency.* The Virginia sub program would never have worked without transparency at all levels and between all the organizations involved in the program— the Navy, Electric Boat, Newport News, and all their suppliers. Information had to flow freely across these organizations, and information technology had a major role in making that possible.

But transparency is as much a behavioral issue as it is a matter of having good technology and good processes. Many companies practice secrecy in their relationships with customers and even within their own walls. Their processes were designed to be opaque, assuming there is something to hide or protect. Today, the Internet enables transparency and actually drives it across companies and between companies and their customers. Some information must, of course, remain proprietary and protected. The Navy has a lot of information that it cannot and will not, for security reasons, share openly. But companies need to open up. The question they need to keep asking themselves is simple and straightforward: Why can't we share this information?

▶ *Find the IT factor.* The saga of the Virginia class subs should be a wake-up call for any company still resisting the use of information technology to raise operational efficiency. The Navy used computer-based simulation, for example, to predict the impact of proposed changes in design or production on a ship's construction schedule. The technique also made it possible to determine the most efficient production pace—efforts to exceed that speed were shown to actually increase costs.

That kind of knowledge is so essential to a company's operational excellence that only penury can excuse the absence of up-to-date technology. Properly applied, these new tools are taking much of the guesswork out of the delivery process. They are providing precisely the information leaders need to make the right decisions.

The Navy's Virginia Class program confirms, once again, that it's technology, process, and people that combine to deliver operational excellence.

BACK IN DECEMBER 1999, JUST IN TIME FOR CHRISTMAS, BOB ARZBAECHER'S BOSS CALLED HIM IN FOR A CHAT. BOB WAS THE CHIEF FINANCIAL OFFICER OF APPLIED POWER, A MANUFACTURER OF INDUSTRIAL AND ELECTRONICS PRODUCTS BASED IN WAUKESHA, WISCONSIN. HIS BOSS WAS RICHARD G. SIM, THE CHAIRMAN AND CHIEF EXECUTIVE. HERE'S HOW BOB DESCRIBES THE ENCOUNTER: "HE TOLD ME HE HAD SOME GOOD NEWS AND SOME BAD NEWS. THE GOOD NEWS WAS THAT I WAS GOING TO GET TO BE THE CEO OF A NEW YORK STOCK EXCHANGE COMPANY. THE BAD NEWS WAS THAT THE COMPANY WAS GOING TO BE LOADED DOWN WITH DEBT."

CHAPTER 4

DOING BETTER EVERY DAY: ACTUANT AIMS AND DELIVERS (AGAIN AND AGAIN)

Applied Power planned to spin off its electronics businesses in a new entity called APW Ltd. As much of the parent company's debt as possible would be dumped on APW, which would operate as the Actuant Corporation—an assortment of outfits manufacturing such products as industrial pumps, electrical tools, and equipment to lift truck cabins.

On July 31, 2000, Bob Arzbaecher became president and chief executive of Actuant. His prospects were far from rosy. The company had sales of $482 million a year, but the debt added up to more than $400 million. He had been ordered to work with the existing heads of the various businesses rather than assembling his own leadership team. And he quickly recognized that his 1,200 employees had "an incredible lack of motivation." They had been summarily cast off as unwanted by their parent company, and now they were part of a much smaller organization with a most uncertain future.

Bob managed to overcome those challenges, and then some. Actuant's debt was drastically shrunk, its sales soared more than fourfold to $1.7 billion, and its employees, now numbering more than 11,000, are highly motivated team players. Actuant products serve industries as varied as shipbuilding, aerospace and defense, oil and gas, railroads, power generation, and agriculture. It is now composed of some 30 companies, most acquired, operating in more than 30 countries. Eighty percent of its revenues comes from products that rank number one in their markets as measured by net sales.

When I asked Bob how all that happened, he offered a formula for delivering that every businessperson should remember: "We looked at what we had, and we tried to make it a little better. We kept our heads down, and we got ourselves a lot of blocking and tackling type first downs." In other words, no razzle-dazzle plays, no wholesale trades of underperformers, no Hail Mary passes—just a calm acceptance of reality and a determined, sustained effort to deliver. "It takes the emotion out of 'Oh, my God, we're inferior,' and gets everyone focused instead on improving," Bob added.

**IN OTHER WORDS, NO RAZZLE-DAZZLE PLAYS, NO WHOLESALE TRADES OF UNDERPERFORMERS, NO HAIL MARY PASSES—JUST A CALM ACCEPTANCE OF REALITY AND A DETERMINED, SUSTAINED EFFORT TO DELIVER.**

Actuant has formalized this commitment with a program it calls LEAD, for Lean Enterprise Across Disciplines. Initially, Bob just urged the business units to try it out; now, it's mandatory, with facilitators being trained in every enterprise. "I don't care if you're 10 people in an office or 250 people in a factory," he says. "You have to have LEAD." In fact, LEAD principles and practices are applied to every project and process across all the company's many business units, and the program is the centerpiece in Actuant's unique approach to integrating newly acquired organizations.

The goal of greater operational efficiency should not be limited to the factory floor. It has a strategic role as well, and Bob Arzbaecher has found a way to incorporate that goal in his company's drive to grow through acquisitions. He relies on a program called AIM, for Acquisition Integration Model, which has had remarkable success in blending more than a score of outside companies into Actuant's distinctive continuous-improvement culture.

As Bob says, and I concur, the main reason so many mergers misfire is not because of a wrong-headed strategy or a flawed due diligence: "The problem is a failure to bring two cultures together quickly, seamlessly, and pragmatically." He knows what he's talking about. "I cut my teeth on acquisitions at an organization that knew how to do them," he told me. A CPA with a 1982 degree in accounting from the University of Iowa, he was part of the hyperactive mergers-and-acquisitions team at Chicago's Farley Industries. And he kept his hand in M&A after joining Applied Power in 1992 as corporate controller.

**As Bob says, and I concur, the main reason so many mergers misfire is not because of a wrong-headed strategy or a flawed due diligence: "The problem is a failure to bring two cultures together quickly, seamlessly, and pragmatically."**

In the pages ahead, I set forth AIM's key integration concepts and techniques, a mini-toolkit that can help you navigate through the thicket that can threaten any merger or acquisition.

First, though, take a closer look at this sprawling conglomerate, whose roots date back 99 years to the founding of the American Grinder and Manufacturing Company in Milwaukee. Its first product was a hand grinder for sharpening tools, but with the arrival of World War I, the company branched out into water pumps for truck engines and other military vehicles. With war's end, the pumps moved to Model T's, and by 1920 the company was also turning out wrenches and other hand tools under the brand name Blackhawk with a silhouette of an a Native American within an arrowhead as its logo.

Five years later, American Grinder renamed itself Blackhawk, and it began collecting more product lines, the building blocks of today's company. The purchase of the Hydraulic Tool Company, a small hydraulic jack manufacturer in Los Angeles, started the company in the business of high-force tools and equipment including industrial pumps and presses. (One recent ballyhooed project: the lifting and lowering of the 45,000-ton roof of China's "Bird's Nest" Stadium in time for the 2008 Olympics.) To aid a snowplow manufacturer to more easily raise and lower plow blades, Blackhawk devised a remote-control hydraulic system, which led the company to develop a variety of hydraulic tools that are used to push, pull, and straighten cars that have been in collisions.

Blackhawk became Applied Power Industries in 1961, and the company started buying up companies that would move it in a whole new direction. Gardner Bender contributed electrical equipment and voltage testers, for example, whereas, after a hostile-takeover battle, the Barry Wright Corporation added vibration control devices for heavy machinery. Everest Electronic Equipment brought components for computers and data communications on board. Soon enough, Applied found itself in the always uncomfortable stance of riding two horses simultaneously—in this case, an old economy nag and a dot. com stallion. In the process of separation, Actuant was born, and Bob Arzbaecher won his CEO stripes—and got the nag.

He took action immediately, divesting some businesses and buying others that complemented Actuant's existing brands. In 2001, for instance, he acquired Dewald Manufacturing, whose systems for the recreational vehicle market fit nicely with Actuant's own manufacture of RV slide-outs. Starting in 2003, and continuing on through 2009, he has added at least one and as many as five organizations to the Actuant stable annually. And along the way, he has enormously expanded the company's global presence: Forty-six percent of sales are now outside North America, primarily in Europe.

How did he manage to fit all these acquisitions into the Actuant culture? "I'm going to use my favorite word again," Bob says. "Evolution." He relied on LEAD, his lean-production model, to raise the operational efficiency of his acquisition-integration model.

At first, he was mainly concerned with such uncomplicated issues as whether the employees of acquired companies had been signed up for the Actuant benefit system. But he also didn't want them to worry that he was going to "trash and burn things." He had learned that lesson in dealing with the angst of his own employees when Actuant was first formed. Back then he visited every company facility and conducted town hall-type meetings. "The key," he explains, "was to let people get their frustrations out and then assure them that our cash flow was going to stay within our own entity and we were going to build this thing together. I wouldn't say they believed me on day one, but they came around over time."

So, the acquisition-integration model included a series of intense, highly structured sessions between teams of senior people from the acquired company and their counterparts on the corporate and divisional levels of Actuant. These two- and three-person teams representing strategy, operations, sales and marketing, human resources, and information technology met over a 90-day period.

Every 30 days, during that time, the teams gathered for a report-out of their progress, and that data went straight to Bob and his top aides. In each category, he looked for specific results. In terms of the financials, for example, he wanted to see the newcomer linked to the Actuant reporting system within the first month. He also expected the AIM participants to determined what kind of training the new arrivals needed.

But aside from resolving the workaday details, Bob sees the process as a way to get the newcomers acquainted with the

Actuant culture and staff, the people they will henceforth be doing business with. He understands that the new people are going to be far more receptive to his message if it's delivered and demonstrated by their peers within the organization rather than by the chief executive.

The message itself is clear: Actuant doesn't buy companies to shutter them and pull out costs. As he puts it, "We tell them that we acquired their company because we saw some value in it, that one plus one will equal three." They also learn that they are expected to play the major role in realizing that added value—by accepting and applying Actuant's version of the lean-production approach, LEAD.

> THE MESSAGE ITSELF IS CLEAR: ACTUANT DOESN'T BUY COMPANIES TO SHUTTER THEM AND PULL OUT COSTS. AS HE PUTS IT, "WE TELL THEM THAT WE ACQUIRED THEIR COMPANY BECAUSE WE SAW SOME VALUE IN IT, THAT ONE PLUS ONE WILL EQUAL THREE."

I had a long talk recently with Dave Buck, one of the six members of the company's LEAD support group. They have all had heavy-duty line positions and lean production experience, and each of them works with five or so business units. "We assist them on their continuous improvement journey," Dave says, "as mentor, consultant, teacher, inspirer." They work directly with the top executive and the LEAD leader of each business unit, and each unit also has a LEAD steering committee. Among other things, Dave and his colleagues help establish training programs to introduce new hires to LEAD and to raise a unit's overall LEAD skill level. "We put in a structure and some tools and strategy," he notes, "but more importantly we drive a culture of continuous improvement. In any business unit, for instance, you want your best people in continuous-improvement leadership positions, because it's all about focusing on a change in the culture, not on the tools."

In the case of a recent executive hire at a business unit, Dave tells me, he spent some 36 hours with the newcomer, one-on-one, laying out Actuant's LEAD process, structure, expectations, and reporting policies. Dave also modeled a few LEAD-oriented events to show how the company expects them to be run and followed up on. And all this for an executive who already had a strong background in continuous-improvement operations.

I asked Dave a question I knew would be tough to answer: "How far has the company as a whole traveled on the continuous-improvement journey?" He thought about it aloud, ticking off various business units. One of them was doing fine: "They're having daily and weekly LEAD meetings with people on the shop floor about making improvements, and they're taking their ideas. Everything is done in a cell. They're never really happy with anything, constantly tweaking it. They're well on the journey." At another business, a woman found a way to trim the space her operation occupied, doing more with fewer people. On the other hand, there were units that were "just awakening to the process." His best estimate: Half of the businesses were really well along on the journey.

Members of the LEAD support group are important players in the intense acquisition-integration process. (One participant compared it to being at the business end of a fire hose.) They make hour-long presentations to the leadership of the acquired company and others to all its employees. Every operational aspect is covered, but the larger goal is to achieve buy-in to the LEAD mission. When that happens, Bob Arzbaecher and his headquarters team can begin to relax and loosen the reins. Dave Buck or another member of the support group, working with the new acquisition's LEAD leader, will always be there pushing for ever-greater progress in continuous improvement, but otherwise the newcomer will be free to pursue its own strategy and tactics.

Meanwhile, headquarters looks after such areas as insurance, treasury, and investor relations, while searching for new ways to leverage the scale and diversity of its huge portfolio of businesses. It's also responsible for broadcasting best practices and new technologies across the whole gamut of companies. On Actuant's intranet, for example, managers can find detailed presentations covering the lean-production tools that are part of the LEAD approach. The intranet also includes a forum for answering particular questions. And if you want to run a total production maintenance event, you can find there the names and contact information for people within Actuant who will talk you through it.

"We don't have an independent R&D center that dreams up products," Bob says proudly. "What we have is a management team that really communicates well and businesses that are willing to help a sister business." One reason the corporate management team can fulfill that mission is its cohesion. In spite of the size of the organization, he explains, "The top 100 people still know each other and still run together. We have a very informal, walk-into-your-office mentality around here."

"WE DON'T HAVE AN INDEPENDENT R&D CENTER THAT DREAMS UP PRODUCTS," BOB SAYS PROUDLY. "WHAT WE HAVE IS A MANAGEMENT TEAM THAT REALLY COMMUNICATES WELL AND BUSINESSES THAT ARE WILLING TO HELP A SISTER BUSINESS."

A major item covered in the AIM sessions with new acquisitions, and a key element of the Actuant culture, is a policy called Feed the Eagles. If you run a business that shows a steady growth in the return on invested capital, on the top line, and on a cash flow basis, you can count on corporate to contribute considerable resources including cash and personnel and greater encouragement to scout for acquisitions to build your market share. "We make no bones about it within the company," Bob tells me. "A lot of companies focus on their problems. We focus on our successes. And it turns out that people really strive harder to better their operations and growth to win the honor, and benefits, of being an eagle."

Bob places a heavy emphasis on the timing of the AIM process. He believes it should commence as soon as the deal to acquire a company is signed. "Think about every time you've taken on a new job," he tells me. "That first 90 days, if you got a bad impression of the place, it takes you years to unwind. The same is true with acquisitions." The goal is to give newcomers a "sense of closure. We really try to celebrate the final day report-out with T-shirts and memorabilia, whatever we can do to make them feel a part of the family."

The acquisition integration program is more or less intense depending on the nature of operations within the company acquired. The degree to which operational efficiencies exist, for example, can vary widely from one takeover to the next. Bob recalls visiting a small business in the Midwest 10 days after it had been purchased. He met with the senior management team and then went out on the factory floor to present a slide show about the LEAD program. When he finished, a woman seated in a back row stood up and asked, "When are we going to get some of that LEAD here, because we are f***d up." The general manager was understandably embarrassed, but Bob replied: "You can start tomorrow. And by the way, I don't look at it that your outfit is f***d up. I look at it that you know you can do better."

As it turned out, the newcomer became an exemplar of the AIM process. The business made the transition to LEAD in no time and completed a top-to-bottom reorganization. Its footprint was so drastically reduced, saving so much working capital, that it was rewarded with a brand new building and given a Golden A award as the company's most improved LEAD business.

The in-depth explorations of the acquisition-integration program can wreak havoc with pre-acquisition assumptions. Bob recalls buying two companies that made torque wrenches to fill a gap in an Actuant business's product line. But at the first AIM meeting, the new companies' leaders announced that selling torque wrenches to oil companies was not the way to go. Their customers were looking for a supplier that would do the actual tensioning and torquing in a joint integrity product—services in addition to the product.

"We came home from that first integration meeting saying, "Man, that's different than we thought!" Bob explains. "We missed it in our due diligence. But we were able to get past our preconceived notions, and we totally changed our organizational direction." So instead of turning the newcomers into a subsidiary of the product company, he put them together as a separate business. It has since added four acquisitions of its own and mushroomed into a $200 million operation.

In 2005, Actuant bought Gits Manufacturing, a 95-year-old company based in Creston, Iowa. It had started out making lubricating devices and oil cups for autos and factory machinery and then moved on to vents for bulk chemical containers. It was now producing air flow devices that increased fuel efficiency and reduced emissions in heavy duty trucks and passenger cars. In the course of the acquisition-integration process, Bob learned that the president of Gits, Daryl Lilly, was a true gearhead who had raced cars for decades and knew everything about how their engines work. Once again, Bob set about making the most of the results of the AIM process.

Actuant built Gits a new research center and put Lilly in charge. The center developed record-breaking tolerances on front-end engine valves despite 1,000-degree temperatures and enormous vibration. Beyond that, Lilly has found a way to cut the delivery time of prototypes from six months to a matter of days. "Daryl gets them to a customer's engineers so fast," Bob notes, "that their purchasing people have to catch up. Meanwhile, the engineers get so hopped up about it they make our product part of their design. You can imagine what that does for our bargaining position on the pricing."

Wherever Actuant acquires a company today, the AIM process is automatically set in motion, and that includes China. The company has been sourcing there for decades, but since 2000, it has been buying businesses to establish and bolster its own engineering, production, and assembly capacity. In July 2008, most of these operations were consolidated in a 300,000-square-foot facility in Hangsu Province.

Acquisitions in China, particularly in the $35- to $50-million range that Actuant favors, are something of a challenge because the M&A market is immature and due diligence is difficult. Bob has relied on AIM to get a thorough sense of the newcomers and bring them into the fold. The integration process was handled by Actuant's senior Chinese cadre. "The language and cultural issues made that necessary," Bob explains, "but be aware that no acquisition would have taken place if I wasn't comfortable that the senior team on the ground was capable of taking on the integration."

Evidence of the value of those AIM sessions emerged when the company brought forth a revolutionary new pump, with a hydraulic delivery 50 percent higher than that of conventional air-over-hydraulic devices. In the past, Actuant would develop such a product within a particular region and then market it worldwide. In this case, the development was on a global basis, shared by engineers in China, Europe, and the United States. It was a project that put a premium on the communication skills and shared culture of the participants, another coup for the company's acquisition-integration process.

As you can see, Bob Arzbaecher applies his make-it-a-little-better mandate to all Actuant's operations, including AIM itself, always endeavoring to do more with less. "Evolution," he says. "That's what we're all about."

# IRRESISTIBLE OBJECT ADAPTS TO IMMOVABLE FORCE

You might think that as the head of Maxima, the multi-billion dollar Actuant business unit that makes vehicle instrumentation, 75-year-old Oddie V. Leopando might already have enough on his plate. No, when we spoke, he was making plans to take part in a 4-hour Six Sigma refresher course at his company's headquarters in Lancaster, Pennsylvania. He's a Six Sigma black belt, and he proudly reported that his new project proposal had just been approved by his teacher. He also assured me that his personal involvement in Six Sigma was "one of the most important things I've ever done for this company."

Back in 2000, years before the Actuant acquisition, CEO Oddie decided that Maxima had to transform its product line from electromechanical to electronic to stay competitive. At the same time, he concluded that something special would be needed to convince customers like C&H and Caterpillar that Maxima could really maintain its quality level in this new dimension. Maxima instruments go into $300,000 machines that operate under extreme conditions, and if the instruments fail, there's hell to pay. The way for the company to prove itself, he determined, was to transform its processes as well—by means of Six Sigma.

"I had to make sure that I was not only the sponsor and champion of the method but a part of it myself," he tells me. "I became a green belt, and I ordered my whole core management team to do the same. Six Sigma would not have succeeded otherwise."

But succeed it did. Two years later, a green belt training class was underway when a group of Caterpillar executives happened to pass by and stopped in to listen. They were mightily impressed, concluding that the Maxima green belt level was the equal of their black belt. It wasn't long thereafter that Caterpillar awarded Maxima a major electronic program, and today the company is a preferred Caterpillar supplier—and a partner in Six Sigma.

When Maxima was acquired in December 2006, Oddie was well aware of Actuant's determined commitment to its AIM acquisition-integration program. But he suggested that he and his top people, rather than an Actuant team, should lead the process at Maxima. His company, he argued, had already been through its own continuous-improvement transformation. And the folks at Maxima agreed. "That was one of the things I liked about them," Oddie tells me. "They weren't rigid."

By having his team of black-belt executives run the AIM process, Oddie achieved their buy-in to the Maxima LEAD mandate, while translating the lean systems the company already had in place into the LEAD model. In effect, Six Sigma became a "super tool" in the LEAD toolbox. "For the kind of smaller, rapid-type improvements we rely on," Bob Arzbaecher says, "LEAD is a better tool than Six Sigma."

One of the things Oddie finds most impressive about Actuant is that it is "very nimble" in sharing new best practices among the business units. He also enjoys the content and openness of leadership meetings. "It's not presentations," he explains, "it's work groups and brainstorming. Voices get raised, but afterward it's all behind you and you're smoking a cigar with Bob. He's made that a part of the culture."

## STAND AND DELIVER

> ▸ *Join the hunt.* At first glance, you might think a global recession would not be a time to think or write about mergers and acquisitions, but think again. The world is full of good businesses struggling and in need of help. Bargains abound. "It's become a buyer's market," Bob Arzbaecher tells me. "We've positioned ourselves with a brand new credit agreement where we can really go after some of those opportunities."

By acquiring the right company, or even companies, you can often boost your total operational skills and create needed change. But be aware that every study of mergers and acquisitions shows that more than half fail to deliver on their promise. As the Actuant story makes clear, both due diligence and smart post-merger management are necessary for success.

▶ *Expect to be surprised.* By now you know that I believe in your having some kind of substantial, in-depth process in place to integrate an acquired company into your operation. There's no other way I know of to ensure that the new company will actually advance your own organization's operational goals. At the same time, the integration process requires a substantial degree of flexibility. For all your due diligence before purchase, you can count on some surprises, both pleasant and otherwise. Actuant learned that lesson with its acquisition of Gits, for example, with its mechanically gifted president. The AIM process ensures the company's ability to spot surprises quickly and manage through them.

▶ *Manage the soft side.* All sorts of technical knots have to be untied when you acquire a company, details that must be addressed to make sure that the integration succeeds on an operational level. But none of that is going to work unless you've managed the human side of the equation. You have to overcome the destructive mix of anxiety, sense of loss, and malaise that so often affects the acquired organization's people. Actuant's AIM process puts a major emphasis on easing these concerns. As Bob puts it, "We tell them, You're no longer in purgatory, you're no longer part of an acquired company, you're now part of Actuant." After the newcomers actually accept their new status, when they embrace the new culture, they start to relax and to entertain the possibility that the future might be even better than the past.

▶ *Accentuate the positive.* Actuant's culture has great appeal because it harnesses the drive to succeed that is a natural part of all of us. The Feed the Eagles policy, for example, captures that part of the culture while also telling the company where to put its resources for the highest payoff. When a company is acquired, AIM acquaints newcomers with this approach. It comes as a surprise to many of them because their previous employers may have relied on threats and fear as their chief motivating factors. The Eagle approach addresses other, more positive parts of their psyches. It speaks to our desire to excel, to win the admiration of our peers, and to share in the rewards of our labors. It's a far more effective, long-term way to inspire people to work harder and better, whether they are veteran employees or newcomers.

▶ *Spread the good word.* Actuant never wastes a good idea by keeping it locked up in one business unit. It moves innovations and best practices across the whole corporation. Sometimes it does that by moving people, and sometimes it just moves ideas though discussions at its executive team meetings. Whatever the mechanism, good ideas need to be highlighted and shared.

▶ *Go lean.* If you want to be competitive in manufacturing today, you better go lean. Companies committed to this continuous, process-focused improvement technique have achieved extremely high levels of efficiency. Each of them has its own approach, but it's possible to draw some wise principles from the way Actuant operates under its LEAD program.

No business should try to change all its work processes at one time. Companies have a limited management capacity, especially for managing change. So apply your lean efforts to those processes that can yield the fastest and best improvement in business performance. Actuant, for instance, heavily focuses LEAD on its engineering processes, creating products so superior that customers' engineers will accept no others.

## No business should try to change all its work processes at one time.

When starting out with lean manufacturing, look for some low-hanging fruit—processes that you can improve quickly. That can help you get the hang of the techniques involved as soon as possible. It can also jump-start your team members' confidence that they can handle the lean technique and that the changes it produces are an improvement.

WHEN STARTING OUT WITH LEAN MANUFACTURING, LOOK FOR SOME LOW-HANGING FRUIT—PROCESSES THAT YOU CAN IMPROVE QUICKLY.

Lean teams, like those at Actuant, should be made of top-notch people who understand your manufacturing processes and recognize the need for substantial change and process improvement. Actuant does it by leveraging, a small cadre of corporate specialists that moves between business units advising and consulting on how to implement lean techniques. The implementation teams are drawn from within the individual businesses, allowing the people who know the operation best to figure out the right solution. Then it's up to the units to run with the program, adapting the techniques to their own conditions, but being sure to get the results that the business needs. There is no single best way to implement a process change program. Let the people "on the ground" figure out the best way to do it, but hold them accountable for the results. And follow the principles articulated here.

LEAN TEAMS, LIKE THOSE AT ACTUANT, SHOULD BE MADE OF TOP-NOTCH PEOPLE WHO UNDERSTAND YOUR MANUFACTURING PROCESSES AND RECOGNIZE THE NEED FOR SUBSTANTIAL CHANGE AND PROCESS IMPROVEMENT.

IF YOU'RE ENMESHED IN A
CORPORATE TURNAROUND, I KNOW
OF NO BETTER PLACE TO LOOK FOR
INSPIRATION THAN THAT AMERICAN
ICON, THE CAMPBELL SOUP
COMPANY. A HUMBLE CAN OF SOUP
IS A DECEPTIVELY SIMPLE IMAGE
FOR A COMPANY WHOSE RECIPE
FOR REVIVAL INCLUDED SOME OF
THE BEST BUSINESS PRACTICES
AROUND. THEY EXPLAIN WHY
CAMPBELL'S AWAKENED FROM WHAT
LOOKED TO SOME LIKE A TERMINAL
SNOOZE.

CHAPTER 5

## GETTING BACK TO FOCUS AND DISCIPLINE: CAMPBELL'S SOUP IS M'M M'M SMART

I've studied the company and its 58-year-old CEO, Douglas R. Conant, for some time now. To ignite a turnaround, he brought to the table two characteristics that are crucial to delivering: focus and discipline. Today, they're what the company is all about.

### TO IGNITE A TURNAROUND, HE BROUGHT TO THE TABLE TWO CHARACTERISTICS THAT ARE CRUCIAL TO DELIVERING: FOCUS AND DISCIPLINE.

When he took over at Campbell's in 2001, Doug Conant promised the company's stakeholders that there would be better times ahead. As of January 2009, total return on Campbell's stock since his arrival, given dividend reinvestment, was 31.5 percent—as compared to the S&P 500's 14.4 percent loss for the same period.

Here's how Doug describes the Campbell's advantage: "The soup business is the largest, most profitable, fastest-turning category in the entire center of a grocery store. We have a leadership position to the point that we are the category manager for every customer in the country. There is no other company of any kind that has that kind of leverage in a category in the United States."

In 2001, though, the company was in the doldrums after one of the most amazing knee-bone-connected-to-the-thigh-bone sequences I've ever encountered. As Doug describes it to me, the downward spiral was kicked off in 1990 or so with the decision to raise prices. Over the next seven years, for example,

the EBIT margin for canned soup more than doubled, creating
a large price differential with supermarket private labels. When
that triggered a sales decline, it was blamed on poor promotion,
and the ad budget was slashed, after which sales took another
hit. By now, earnings were hurting, so the company embarked
on a major cost-cutting campaign, up to and including a
reduction in the amount of chicken in Campbell's chicken
noodle soup.

At that point, as Doug puts it, "After taking the pricing up,
cutting the marketing support, and compromising on product
quality, we started to cut the overhead including hundreds of
R&D people, the lifeblood of a consumer-products company. By
then, 9 out of 10 of the best people left on their own." Between
1997 and 2000, sales of condensed soup, which accounted for
more than half of Campbell's soup sales, dropped by more than
20 percent.

Within the ranks, inertia ruled. A former executive recalls,
only half in jest, that she used to carry a mirror to "make sure
everyone was breathing." When someone proposed that
less heat in the cooking process would improve the soup's
texture and flavor, the notion was vetoed; retooling for the
change would have cost $100 million. But then, when the rival
Progresso brand, owned by General Mills, pioneered the lower-
heat process, Campbell's was forced to follow—and the net
result was that it spent the money anyway, but lost the edge of
being first.

Turning this ship around would be a challenge for anyone,
and there were those who doubted that Doug Conant could

do it despite his 25 years as an executive in the food business. Born in Chicago, he received both his BA and MBA at nearby Northwestern University. There his professors included Philip Kotler, whom Doug describes as "the godfather of consumer marketing as we know it today." Kotler pioneered brand management." He went straight into brand management at General Mills after graduation and then on to Kraft, where Doug said he was "turned on to the whole concept." Then it was on to Nabisco, which had just gone through its notorious leveraged buyout. He was president of Nabisco when Campbell's came calling.

But Doug is a far cry from the classic extrovert-on-steroids CEO. He calls himself an introvert who needs his "alone time," dislikes chit-chat with strangers, and vacations in places like the mountains of Utah or the Michigan woods for tranquil reflection. Doug reads at least four hours a day, largely books of management advice, making use of the long commute from his home in northern New Jersey to Campbell's headquarters, the length of the state away in Camden, near Philadelphia. He keeps scores of books in his office, on shelves and stacked in corners. And when he finds one he likes, he buys extra copies and hands them out to his colleagues. He greets both triumph and disaster with quiet self-possession. One of his colleagues calls him "an Eagle scout."

But Doug Conant is no pushover. He has had his share of hard knocks, including the loss of his job as head of marketing for Parker Brothers when General Mills decided to get out of the toy and games business. Doug was out of work for a year, a turning point in his life, he says. When he re-launched at Kraft, he was ready to learn the hard disciplines of cutting costs, trimming staff, launching new products, and revamping marketing plans. He turned around the margarine division and then the Planters and Life Savers brands.

In his first months at Campbell's, Doug moved decisively with similar focus and discipline. Convinced that most of the executives he inherited were at Campbell's only because they couldn't find other jobs, he began to replace them, eventually firing fully 300 of the company's 350 top people. One of the greatest weaknesses of the company as he found it, Doug tells me, was its focus on quarter-by-quarter earnings. It had taken long years to get into trouble, and he knew it would take long years to get out of it. He lowered earnings expectations and slashed the dividend by 30 percent. As he expected, the stock plummeted, hardly manna for the Dorrance family, heirs of the Campbell chemist who invented condensed soup, who still control about half of the company's shares. But they backed his play, which was designed to free up funds for long-term growth and innovation. Jim Kilts, the one-time Gillette CEO who was Doug's boss and mentor at Nabisco, calls him "the guy with an iron fist in a velvet glove."

As a long-term turnaround strategy, Doug limned a 10-year plan he called "the Campbell's Journey." It focused on changing the corporate culture and embracing mission-driven innovation. In the first phase, 2001 through 2004, the company would regain its competitiveness by upgrading the management team, increasing employee engagement, and working on innovative product improvements. In the next three years, Campbell's would achieve quality growth by enhancing the overall value proposition for customers. And beginning in 2008, the plan predicted the company would chalk up unprecedented rates of growth and become nothing less than "the world's most extraordinary food company."

The first and biggest transformation Doug had to make at Campbell's was to reform the sluggish culture. "We had to win in the workplace," he tells me, "so we could ultimately win in the marketplace." That was a monstrous task, given its 23,000-person payroll, but Doug saw no alternative. A new product or technology can give you an edge, but it would be fleeting. He understood that the real competitive advantage is the ability, the agility, and the willingness of your workforce to cope with dynamic markets and situations.

THE FIRST AND BIGGEST TRANSFORMATION DOUG HAD TO MAKE AT CAMPBELL'S WAS TO REFORM THE SLUGGISH CULTURE. "WE HAD TO WIN IN THE WORKPLACE," HE TELLS ME, "SO WE COULD ULTIMATELY WIN IN THE MARKETPLACE."

In turning the Campbell culture around, Doug used a concept developed by the Gallup Group called the Engagement Ratio—a measure of how many employees are fully engaged in their jobs. According to Gallup, to have a team dedicated to the company vision and mission of total customer satisfaction, the majority of the employees must be fully engaged. To reach world-class levels of productivity and efficiency, there must be 12 engaged people for every indifferent one. Doug says Campbell's engagement ratio in 2003 was no better than 2 to 1.

He began by upgrading his management team, establishing a leadership standard against which every executive could be judged. Over his first two years, six out of seven top executives failed to measure up and departed. Significantly, however, he replaced at least half of them with company insiders, sending a positive signal amid the mayhem. The other half he recruited from blue-chip packaged-goods companies, go-getters who wanted to have "a little Don Quixote in their lives" by tilting against the windmills that were crippling the grand old brand.

Doug encouraged a group of employees to draw up the so-called Campbell's Promise, which established the basic equation the company has sought to live by ever since: "The company values its people, and its people value the company." But to begin with, he understood, Campbell would have to "tangibly demonstrate" its side of the equation. Soon, leaders' evaluations were based, in part, on the grades they received from the people who worked with them.

On a personal level, Doug has gone to great pains to show how much he values the associates, as he calls employees. He emcees an annual awards ceremony to honor staffers' accomplishments and ideas. Every six weeks, he has lunch with about a dozen employees to get their feedback and advice. In business, he says, "We're trained to find things that are wrong, but I try to celebrate what's right." And he sets aside time every day to send hand-written notes of appreciation to staffers who have delivered in extraordinary ways, from executive vice presidents to the receptionist at a remote field office. In his first eight years at Campbell's, more than 16,000 thank-you notes went out. "I'm 'all in' in terms of moving this company forward," he tells me, "and every associate gets it. You can ask any one of them and they would say, 'He's all in.'"

Doug also generates engagement and improves operations by deflecting praise and sharing credit. He has the discipline to own up readily to his mistakes, saying simply, "I can do better." In a conference call with Wall Street analysts early in 2009, for instance, he came under fire for not fighting harder when retailers cut their inventories of soup, presenting at least some shoppers with bare shelves. Doug acknowledged that it had been a "frustrating experience," and that in hindsight both he and the retailers would have behaved differently. "We were up eight percent in the first half," he says. "And quite frankly, it should have been more. I wish it was, and it wasn't. But I am not embarrassed by eight percent growth."

Campbell Soup employees also appreciate the company's commitment to sustainability and corporate social responsibility—one of the seven "core strategies" that Doug set out for the company early on. "We had been making some compromises no one felt good about," he tells me. "Now, we decided that we were going to win with integrity."

Doug sponsored green initiatives at Nabisco long before they were fashionable. He has always been a "forward thinker," according to his former boss Kilts. At Campbell's, he promised sustainable farm and manufacturing practices. Campbell's also has a major commitment to Camden, the economically depressed industrial city where it was founded. It is now building a $70 million corporate campus there and has a dozen or more programs to educate and train the city's young people, prepare renters for home ownership, revitalize neighborhoods, support health clinics, and provide meals, job search assistance, and health services for the needy.

As a result of all these patient efforts throughout the company, the engagement ratio at Campbell's climbed to 9 to 1 in 2007. And in July 2008, Doug proudly announced that the ratio had hit "a world-class 12 to 1," and that the Gallup Group "has recognized Campbell's as one of the best places to work in America in each of the last two years."

While the culture at Campbell's was being transformed, of course, the rest of the business couldn't sit still. Doug decreed that it would be based on four pillars that he considers "musts" for any food enterprise: quality, value, convenience, and wellness (healthy nutrition). It was obvious that Campbell's had a long road to travel in each category. "You can't talk your way out of something you behaved your way into," Doug told his troops. "You have to behave your way out of it." Campbell's would have to learn to do more with less. Following are the problems, and the focus and discipline, he used to address them:

> ▶ At a time when consumers increasingly focused on health issues—more than 65 million Americans suffer from hypertension—wellness was perhaps Campbell's most pressing concern. Sales of the staple condensed soup were dropping at least partly because customers worried about its high levels of sodium and flavor-enhancing monosodium glutamate (MSG). But repeated efforts to

market low-sodium soups had been stymied by their bland, unappealing taste.

That problem was finally solved when the Campbell's research labs found a sea salt with relatively little sodium, making possible full-flavored low-sodium soups. The line was the hottest new supermarket product of the year when it came out in 2007, hitting sales of $101 million. These days, low-sodium soup accounts for $650 million in annual sales, and Doug says that one day soon, sodium will be a nonissue in all the company's soups.

The war over MSG has gone even better. The battle was joined when rival Progresso ran ads taunting Campbell's about its sodium and flavor-enhancer addictions. Campbell's waited until its products caught up with its wellness goals and retaliated with a campaign boasting that 124 of its soups were MSG-free, whereas Progresso was loaded with the stuff. Within a few years, Doug maintains, there won't be MSG in any Campbell soups.

The nonsoup brands were part of what he calls the "better-for-you" commitment. V8 branched out into citrus mixtures and, with V Fusion, a full serving of fruit plus a full serving of vegetables in every glass, offering vitamins A, C, and E with no added sugar. The Pepperidge Farm brand switch to whole grain baked goods has been "wildly successful," Doug says. Campbell's also moved strongly into organic products. The 2008 acquisition of the Wolfgang Puck line of organic soups gave the company further breadth and credibility in the organic market and an opening to many potential entries in natural foods.

▶ For Doug's second pillar, quality, read upscale marketing—a field Campbell's started to plow with its ready-to-serve Chunky line of soups well before he arrived. Chunky has been upgraded, with quality ingredients and lean meat, and promoted heavily with an ad campaign featuring NFL running back LaDanian Tomlinson. The line is also being beefed up with two extension brands, Healthy Request and Fully Loaded.

The Select Harvest and Wolfgang Puck lines add to Campbell's upscale offerings, and its Swanson line is adding beef and chicken stock aimed to help gourmet cooks enrich their sauces. The company has also tested a line of refrigerated soups with gourmet flavors, such as crab and sweet corn chowder, to be sold at premium prices—perhaps $5.50 for 24 ounces, compared to about $2.50 for 19 ounces of Chunky soup.

Perhaps surprisingly, Doug recently sold off an upscale brand that had been doing well: Godiva chocolates. His admirers give him full credit for recognizing that however hip the brand and its $500 million in sales seemed, the company would do better to focus on its core business.

▶ Convenience, Doug's third "must," was the original selling point for condensed soup: Just add water, heat, and serve. In the fast-food age, however, that process no longer seemed simple enough. Ready-to-serve soups were more convenient, especially when Campbell's began packaging them in pop-top cans. And under Doug, the company finally saw potential in the microwave oven. "The microwave was invented in 1947," he marvels, "but we were so good at putting soup in cans that it took us until 2002 to put it into a microwaveable container. Meanwhile, we lost a whole generation of people who weren't interested in making a can of soup."

Convenience is also an issue in supermarkets, where it's often difficult to find the soup you're looking for on crowded shelves. Research shows that shoppers get impatient if they can't find an item in 20 seconds, but it was taking more than a minute for them to locate the Campbell's flavor they wanted. The company came up with an answer in the form of gravity-fed racks that deliver one can after another to the front of the rack, each flavor in its own well-marked line. As of early 2009, the racks had been installed in 23,000 stores.

▶ The final pillar, value, has also been a constant for Campbell's, and it looks especially good in a time of rising unemployment, worried homemakers, and pinched pennies. Prices of most food items have risen sharply since 2003, but a serving of Campbell's condensed soup has gone up by only nine cents; you can savor a bowl for just 52 cents. Since the recession struck, Doug says, he has "opportunistically" increased advertising for condensed as "the original dollar menu" and, with a Kraft grilled-cheese sandwich, a "wallet friendly" meal. As Campbell's most popular soup, condensed is the company's anchor to windward in this economic storm.

On the way to delivering "the world's most extraordinary food company," Doug means to stay focused on his core business of soup. There are already six cans in the typical U.S. household, and Campbell's soups are sold in 120 countries around the globe, but to Doug, plenty of room exists for expansion. With $3.5 billion of its $8 billion annual sales in soup, he says, Campbell's is the world's largest soup company—but it's still competing in just 6 percent of the world's soup markets. So the company is moving to enter the two largest markets in the world, accounting together for half of all the soup sold: China and Russia. Americans consume 15 billion servings of soup a year, compared to the Russians' 32 billion and China's 300 billion. As another Campbell's executive jokes, the Russians and the Chinese "are professional soup eaters and the rest of us are part-timers."

Campbell's did both extensive and intensive research into the two markets, even sending ethnographers to live with families and probe their eating and cooking habits. It soon became clear that in both countries, soup is central to cooking and intensely personal to the cooks—a fact that explained why earlier attempts to market ready-to-serve and even condensed soups had gone nowhere. The new strategy: Sell broths, some of them containing large chunks of meat and vegetables, that home cooks could use as a base for their own distinctive finished soups. As President Larry McWilliams of Campbell International explains, this provides a short-cut that saves a homemaker at least two hours of soup-making time, but the result "is still Mom's finished soup, with Campbell's simply giving her a helping hand." That's another classic example of a smart company focusing on real conditions and having the discipline to deliver what the market wants and needs.

Campbell's Russian brand is *Domashnaya Klassica* (home classics), in basic flavors so far of chicken, beef, and mushroom. Promotion is built around a *domovoy*, the mythical elf who lives in every Russian household and looks after the family. "Our *domovoy* is a very skeptical rascal, who is horrified to learn that his Mom is going to use broth from a pouch," McWilliams explains. Naturally, the elf is reassured and converted after a taste of the soup.

In China, where Shanghai alone matches the entire U.S. market for soup, Campbell's is marketing similar broths under the Swanson label (*Siyongsong* in Mandarin). In both China and Russia, the brand launchings have featured lots of in-store samplings and cooking demonstrations—good marketing tactics for any company introducing a new concept. And in both markets, says Doug, the launches have been successful, and consumers are coming back for more. "We're getting great traction," he notes. "We're bullish about it."

It remains to be seen how the current slump in Russia and reduced growth in China will affect these bold ventures. Whatever the outcome, Doug insists that the company is in both markets for the long haul.

By one count, the company has come through 28 recessions and the Great Depression in its 139 years; it sells to 85 percent of American households, and many of them are already serving more soups—and substituting soups for costlier items, both in lunchboxes and at home, where more people are taking their meals as fewer go to restaurants. "There will not be a recession in eating," according to Harry Balzer, a market researcher with the NPD Group in Port Washington, New York. "There will only be winners and losers."

Doug predicts that Campbell's will be one of the winners, but he is, as usual, realistic. He reminded me of a day in the fall of 2008 when 499 of the S&P 500 stocks were down; only Campbell's was up. "That was because people were thinking we had the perfect recession food," he says, adding, "Well, it's good but not perfect. And the marketplace is too frenetic. We've had to manage our cost differently, our pricing and quarterly spending differently." He has also had to temporarily manage expectations—"down from 'this is the best thing since sliced bread' to 'this is going to be a very productive company.'" Still, because Doug Conant has built the company for the long term, I have every confidence that expectations will soon, once again, be on the rise.

## STAND AND DELIVER

▶ *Start with a vision and a plan and recognize that success won't come overnight.* There is much to admire and emulate in Doug's presentation of a 10-year plan, "The Campbell's Journey," for getting Campbell's out of the soup. It announced that the new boss recognized that the turnaround was going to take a while, and that employees were not expected to transform themselves and their company overnight. It let them know that he would do whatever it took to win their full participation. And it showed them an inspiring vision of the future along with a roadmap for getting there.

The plan's initial focus on innovation spoke to the apprehensions of all the company's stakeholders. Employees and shareholders alike had watched Campbell's rivals gain ground and even overtake the company with new products and technologies. If the new CEO was going to devote serious resources into research and development, that only made sense. It signaled the kind of forward-looking willingness to deliver that had been lacking for so many years.

By emphasizing the value proposition Campbell's offered customers in the second phase of the plan, Doug was alerting employees, long accustomed to the company's insular ways, to his outward-facing focus—while, at the same time, alerting retailers to his intention to make life better for them and their customers, the consumers.

With his plan, Doug showed employees an inspiring vision of the future along with a roadmap to get there. And they responded. One of the key lessons of the Campbell's transformation is this: It took a lot of energy, intelligence, and persistence on everyone's part, but it all started with a substantive vision and a plan.

▶ *Layoff the cultural misfits.* On the face of it, Doug Conant's decision to dismiss 300 of Campbell's 350 top people may seem extreme, even though he first gave them a chance to prove themselves over many months. But drastic action was needed to right the company. What ails many organizations is the commitment of current management to dysfunctional behaviors and to discredited ways of doing things. Often, that commitment is so strong that it is virtually impossible for its believers to embrace new ways of operating. They offer a dozen reasons for the company's troubles, ranging from unlucky choices to macroeconomic forces, without recognizing that, as Lucy told Charlie Brown, "The whole trouble with you is that you're you!" The weight of disapproval and foot-dragging such employees can bring to bear on a turnaround is enough to bury it. They cannot be happy under a drastically new regime. It is often a hard decision, because these people may have served the company well in past years. But the action is clear: They must go.

▶ *Get clear on how to deliver more to customers.* It's easier to find ways to make a company more efficient that it is to add revenues to its top line. It takes ingenuity to figure out how to grow a business. It just takes discipline to shrink costs. But Conant clearly saw what it would take to deliver more value to consumers and get the company back on track. He would focus on quality, convenience, and wellness, and he would have programs to accomplish each of these objectives.

Conant's vision for Campbell's was not just a set of content-free words that could apply to any company. He set specific objectives that were easily understood and actionable by people inside the company. Consumers would experience more value through quality, convenience, and wellness.

The best objectives for delivering more value to customers are those that build on a company's brand and can realistically leverage a company's capabilities. Conant was pushing Campbell's, but he was always well aware of what the company could actually deliver. Delivering more to customers wasn't an abstract idea. Conant was clear about what to do, and he made sure everyone else was as well. How will you do the same?

▶ *Share the benefits.* Although I have always believed that customers come first, other stakeholders—your shareholders, in particular—can't be ignored. Conant saw ways to deliver more to investors by growing his business in new markets, with a particular emphasis on China and Russia. Entering new markets sometimes requires only a small amount of incremental resources. Other times, much more is required. New markets can be slow to develop. Also, consumers may have different tastes, to which you will have to adapt your product, as Conant experienced. Don't underestimate the resources you will need to grow.

▶ *Turn the page.* For any leader involved in a turnaround, tough decisions are an everyday occurrence. By definition, change only occurs by making a clean break with the past.

During the Campbell's turnaround, Doug took three actions that strike me as best practices for anyone looking to deliver big improvements. Probably it would be too much to call his behavior brave, but see what you think.

Early on, he cut the dividend, and as he expected, the stock plunged. The markets buzzed with negative reactions and predictions. Doug didn't enjoy all that, but he obviously was not surprised. He had a vital goal in mind, to find some cash to put into innovation and growth, and he wasn't about to let the analysts and Wall Street naysayers decide how he went about his business. He was preparing his company for the long term, and he was ready to take whatever short-term criticism came his way.

In December 2007, Doug agreed to sell Godiva to a Turkish holding company for $850 million. The chocolatier had been doing very well, contributing handsomely to profits, but Doug wasn't happy. Godiva was an outlier in the Campbell's list of 20 brands. It took resources away from the core business. Once again, the critics' chorus was heard. Once again, Doug ignored it.

In mapping the company's course in 2001, he had set its ultimate mission as the delivery of long-term value to shareholders, and he had analyzed the companies in the S&P food group to see which had the best record in that regard. He found that the top performers were not those running 60 brands ("things that looked like the U.S. Postal Service") but those that focused on their core products ("the Federal Expresses of the world"). He bet Campbell's future on the second option.

My third example is probably the bravest—and rarest—of all. When he makes a mistake, Doug Conant admits it. He doesn't pretend it didn't happen. He doesn't blame it on 10 other people. He essentially acknowledges failure and promises he'll do better. A trait of a truly great leader is that they understand that they, too, can cause problems.

## A TRAIT OF A TRULY GREAT LEADER IS THAT THEY UNDERSTAND THAT THEY, TOO, CAN CAUSE PROBLEMS.

No one can avoid missteps in a turnaround. So many people are involved in so many changes, big and little, that error is inevitable. Admitting a mistake is admitting you are human. Under some definitions of leadership, still encountered, that is the worst mistake at all: Leaders are supposed to be above blame and reproach. Once they are reduced to human dimensions, so the theory holds, they lose their authority. In fact, just the opposite happens: A human dimension enhances a person's ability to lead.

Today, it is becoming ever more evident that the future of most companies lies with the experience and ingenuity of its people, not within the brain stems of the top management echelon. Leaders who can best tap that great resource and inspire a company to deliver are not authoritarians; they are people like Doug Conant who are sensitive to the needs and desires of his employees, who treat them more as partners than as serfs—and who admit to making mistakes.

You may have noticed that such behavior is not only a matter of bravery. It also just makes sense.

MENTION AN UPSCALE WINERY IN CALIFORNIA'S SONOMA COUNTY—SAY, CLOS DU BOIS—AND WHAT COMES TO MIND? CHANCES ARE IT'S RICH, MELLOW WINES, LOVINGLY HAND-CRAFTED BY PATIENT ARTISANS WHO TRIM THE VINES, HARVEST THE GRAPES A BUNCH AT A TIME, SELECT PRECISELY THE RIGHT BLEND FOR PRESSING AND FERMENTING, AND AGE THE ELIXIR IN OAK BARRELS UNTIL IT'S PERFECT ON THE PALATE. THAT IMAGE IS THE WINE MAKER'S MARKETING MAGIC, AND MUCH OF IT—ESPECIALLY THE MELLOWNESS OF THE WINE—IS SPOT ON. BUT IN TRUTH, CLOS DU BOIS IS ALSO A PRIME EXAMPLE OF A BUSINESS THAT HAS ACHIEVED MAJOR EFFICIENCIES WITHOUT SACRIFICING QUALITY.

CHAPTER 6

## LEVERAGING QUALITY: CLOS DU BOIS COMBINES ELEGANCE AND EFFICIENCY

Frank Woods, the founder of Clos du Bois, never intended to get into wine making. A onetime Procter & Gamble executive who led the development of the Breckenridge ski resort, Woods was looking for a summer home near San Francisco when he found Sonoma County's Alexander Valley. The house he liked there had a vineyard, and Woods thought he could sell the grapes to nearby wineries. He did that for several years, rounding up investors, buying more land, and planting grapes, until his vineyards totaled 520 acres.

But then, in 1974, hard times hit California's wineries. The vintner friend who had contracted to buy Woods's grapes warned him that he had no money and would have to break the contract. But after Woods had tried and failed to find other buyers, his friend offered an alternative: He would make the grapes into wine and store it for a year, giving Woods a chance to market his own label.

By this time, Woods was interested. He had made a tour of the wineries of France with a highly knowledgeable guide and was developing his own palate for wine. At the time, most California wines were selling for $1 to $3 a bottle, but he foresaw that a premium market would develop for the state's vintages, and he decided to lead the way with a $5 bottle.

Woods wanted his wine to have the savor of a good French vintage, but without the tannins that make French wines harsh and difficult to appreciate in their early years. Although the typical California wine was rich, fruity, and robust, Woods's wine would be mellow and approachable. He would avoid the temptation of producing extreme, dramatic wines for connoisseurs. In his own words, his wine would be "universally likeable."

But achieving that vision wasn't easy. Woods was stuck with thousands of gallons of young wine, in vats that would have to be emptied in time for production of his friend's 1975 vintage. He had just a few short months to survey the market, write a business plan, find someone to bottle the wine, and sell the stuff.

He was going to call his wine "Woods Vineyards," but his wife and children vetoed that as too pedestrian. "Clos du Bois," the French equivalent, seemed more upscale; and despite his misgivings about Americans stumbling over the pronunciation, it was adopted. Woods and a friend designed elegant labels for his first three varietal wines—pinot noir, chardonnay, and cabernet sauvignon—in bright colors with a leaf of the cabernet sauvignon grape, like a fleur-de-lis, as the motif. Among the drab labels of the day, they stood out.

Woods' marketing strategy was both bold and innovative. Lacking money for advertising, he sold the wines aggressively at restaurants and clubs, on the theory that customers would see them on wine lists and reason that if the restaurant had chosen Clos du Bois, it must be good. Confident of the quality of his wines, he entered every wine competition he could find, and by the early 1980s had more medals than any other California winery. That impressed *Wine Spectator* magazine, which ran a laudatory article. Finally, Woods chose his distributors carefully and spent a lot of time educating their sales representatives about the virtues of Clos du Bois and how to sell it. He was an early user of shelf cards, those seemingly hand-written notes that hang in front of the bottles describing the taste and best food pairings of the wine.

Woods sold 3,000 cases of Clos du Bois in its first year, 1975, unloading the rest of his stock on the bulk market. Sales doubled in each of the next two years, and Clos du Bois built its own modest winery and tasting room. Woods discovered the velvety smoothness of the merlot grape, and began producing and selling a cabernet-merlot blend with a distinctive blue label. The wine took off, and by 1985 he was selling 60,000 cases of it annually, making him the world's largest merlot producer. He developed a subsidiary brand, River Oaks, to tap into the mass market with his surplus production, and several premium labels (Marlstone and Calcaire, among others) for his highest-quality wines.

All told, Clos du Bois was selling 200,000 cases a year by the mid-1980s. It had been making profits since its third year in business. But all the profit, plus more investment, was being plowed back into the business. Woods figured that to get to a volume of 500,000 cases a year, he would need a capital investment of $20 to $40 million. His search for long-term investment led him to the Hiram Walker brand. And when Allied-Domecq, its owner, made him an offer he couldn't refuse, he didn't. Clos du Bois became part of Allied in 1988. Then it was sold to Beam Wine Estates and, in 2008, to Constellation Wines.

Through all these changes, however, Clos du Bois' managers have hewed to Frank Woods' original vision of the brand, its quality, its positioning in the market, and its mystique. For years, Clos du Bois grew all its own grapes, a fact that impressed its customers so much that even though the brand is now one of the biggest buyers of grapes in California, many people still think of it as a boutique vineyard. And all Clos du Bois wines are still blended to Woods's elegant-but-accessible standard. At the many tasting competitions, judges would compliment him, saying that although many of his competitors had one or two very good wines in the contest, all the wines at his table were exceptional. That lesson isn't lost on Erik Olsen, the brand's wine master since 2003, who still follows the Woods doctrine.

From the beginning, and as noted earlier, Woods was determined to over-deliver on quality, making his wine stand out at every price point it occupied. But he knew that he could achieve that goal in large part by being efficient, keeping costs down, and quality up. For his first winery, he put up not an expensive chateau-like country estate, but an overgrown tin shed near some railroad tracks. Later, a tasting room was tucked into a corner of the warehouse.

Early on, Woods began experimenting with mechanized harvesting of his grapes. Although the machines were devastating to old vines, they worked perfectly well when vines were planted far enough apart and cultivated to accommodate mechanical picking. After mechanized harvesting, other equipment gently separates leaves and debris from the grapes, and the quality of the wine is unaffected. Hand-picking is still done for premium grapes, but as recently as 2008, Clos du Bois had just 80 workers in its winery and 10,000 acres of vineyards, with 50 more people added for the harvest—and they turned out two million cases of wine.

Some technological innovations actually improve the quality of the wine while raising efficiency. When Clos du Bois installed a high-speed bottling line, Erik says, it raised maximum production from 120 bottles a minute to 350 bottles, cutting the bottling cost in half. "Because the equipment is so much better, the quality of the job was greatly improved," he tells me. "Perhaps the biggest enemy of wine is oxygen. The high speed line was much better at keeping dissolved oxygen levels low, and that means that you're going to have more fruit in your wine, and the wine won't age as quickly."

High-speed image technology also supplies efficient quality control. Cameras literally monitor the corking and labeling of every bottle, sounding alarms if a cork is improperly inserted or a label is crooked and shunting the faulty bottle aside. Other cameras make sure each case is fully packed.

Time was when, after fermenting, wine would have to sit in its tanks for several weeks while sediment and particulates settled to the bottom. When centrifuges were first used instead, most wine makers saw them as invidious, whipping up the wine and ruining it by introducing oxygen. But now, Erik says, "They're very gentle. There's no oxygen brought into the wine stream at all." Clos du Bois's new high-speed centrifuge saves three to four percent of total costs—the equivalent of 80,000 cases of wine. Like the filtration technology Erik has introduced, the centrifuge also cuts the amount of wine lost in the processing and increases the clarity of the finished wine. Perhaps most important, it saves two weeks of processing time, which means the wine can stay in barrels longer and develop more quality.

Barrels are vital at Clos du Bois—fully 85,000 of them. As at other premium wineries, red wines are aged in oak barrels; and unlike other wineries, Clos du Bois has fermented its chardonnay in barrels ever since Frank Woods' day. Barrel fermenting, as French vintners have long known, gives chardonnay a depth and character not found in wines that never get out of stainless steel tanks and glass bottles. And after the fermentation is complete, Clos du Bois chardonnay is aged for six to nine months in clean barrels, gaining more depth and complexity.

Clos du Bois's barrels are all made of expensive French oak. Each barrel spends its first three years producing chardonnay, and the next five years aging Clos du Bois's red wines, before being sold off to less discriminating wineries. Computers keep track of the barrels' service record, making it possible to reuse them and thus economize on their cost without compromising quality.

Barrel-fermented chardonnay appealed to the customers; whether they could taste the difference. As Erik put it, "People felt like they were getting something boutiquey and of high quality." But the process was also inefficient, requiring that barrels be stacked and unstacked multiple times as workers cleaned them, inserted grape juice and yeast, and then drained out the fermented wine and cleaned the barrels again. So in 1991, with a nod to Henry Ford, the winery decided to bring the barrels to the workers, running them along a conveyor belt assembly line for the cleaning and filling process and again for the draining and cleaning. It saved untold hours of work and cut down on spillage, too. "This is an old-world process," Erik says, "exactly the same as a boutique winery would use, but much more efficient." Now Clos du Bois has four of the barrel lines.

Quality is built into the Clos du Bois culture; all employees have authority and accountability. The winery is immaculate and scrupulously organized, with every tool and part in its place—a practice that Erik says saves one to two hours a day that employees would otherwise spend looking for fittings. Clos du Bois celebrates each new award with a glass of the winning wine for everyone, and there's a full afternoon party at the winery at the end of every harvest. "If you involve everybody and make them part of the solution," Erik notes, "then they buy into it."

And that focus on quality extends to the top of the corporate ladder. Chris Fehrnstrom, who supervises Clos du Bois for Constellation Wines, recalls presenting a new economizing technique to the corporate board in Rochester, New York. A few minutes into the proposal, chairman Richard Sands stopped him. "You're talking about bringing costs down," he said, "but what I want to understand is, how are you keeping quality the same or improving it while you're cutting costs?" It was a powerful message, and it resonates through the organization.

"YOU'RE TALKING ABOUT BRINGING COSTS DOWN," HE SAID, "BUT WHAT I WANT TO UNDERSTAND IS, HOW ARE YOU KEEPING QUALITY THE SAME OR IMPROVING IT WHILE YOU'RE CUTTING COSTS?"

Constellation Wines has dozens of labels, organized into three divisions. Clos du Bois is part of the mid-priced group, called Vine One, of which Chris is president. And he says data and solutions from the Constellation laboratory help Clos du Bois deliver on its quality promise. Clos du Bois also benefits from using Constellation's purchasing leverage in buying barrels, corks, glass, dry goods, and the like, and the parent company's leverage with distributors in negotiating contracts and profit margins.

Clos du Bois uses the Internet to get closer to its ultimate customers. Selling wine directly to consumers on any large scale is both inefficient and legally complicated, Chris says, so direct Internet sales are probably unlikely any time soon. But communicating with consumers is both possible and desirable, and the winery is pushing into social networking and texting to keep them up to date on its new vintages, its prizes, and its concern for the environment. Closdubois.com now includes an Erik Olsen blog.

Somewhere, there is a limit to how big a winery can grow without compromising its quality or losing its artisan mentality. "We're debating that right now," Chris tells me. There's no question, he explains, that the winery's processes can be scaled up and that the staff's focus on quality is sustainable. The question is whether Clos du Bois can find enough grapes of the caliber it needs to keep growing indefinitely. One option is to keep expanding until a grape-supply ceiling is hit; the other is to keep production near present levels and raise prices. "We're going through that discussion now," he says. "We haven't arrived at the answer yet."

My own bet would be that Clos du Bois will find ways to keep growing and delivering without sacrificing the mellow elegance that wine drinkers have come to count on.

# STAND AND DELIVER

▶ *Efficiency supports quality.* In the popular mind, there is a disconnect between efficiency and quality—a feeling that truly competent, cost-conscious companies can't deliver truly premium goods or services. Quality is held to be synonymous with hand-crafted, painstaking care, which is thought to rule out operational efficiency and assumes high costs. The truth, of course, is that efficiency can—and should—go hand-in-hand with superior quality. As the tale of Clos du Bois so clearly demonstrates, developing ever more proficient, less costly processes delivers financial savings that can then be applied to developing and maintaining ever more superior products.

Particularly in an economic downturn, there's a strong temptation to make cost-cutting a goal in and of itself, divorced from the mission of the company as a whole. Forget it. Every aspect of the company should be viewed as contributing to the larger goal of providing the right product to the customer. Savings that interfere with that goal are counterproductive; savings that are not used to further that goal are wasted.

When Frank Woods and his successors introduced cost-
saving innovations, from mechanized harvesting to
high-speed centrifuges and cameras to the ingenious
barrel-cleansing line, they were often dismissed by
other vintners as efficiency at the cost of quality. They
claimed that mechanized harvesting, for example, would
ruin the grapes, but Woods experimented with different
approaches and found one that kept the grapes intact
while realizing huge overhead savings. His decision to set
up his first winery in a tin shed was typical of that same
determination to hold down costs while over-promising
quality.

▶ *Efficiency improves quality.* Yes, Clos du Bois invests
the money it realizes from its operational efficiencies
in improved product quality, but it has also achieved
the production equivalent of turning lead into gold: It
has created efficiencies that not only cut costs but also
directly improve quality. Its faster bottling technology,
for example, while saving money, also reduced the wine's
exposure to oxygen, creating a fruitier taste and allowing a
slower aging process. When Clos du Bois installed high-
speed centrifuges, it reduced the time required for older
sediment processes and increased the amount of time that
wine could age in oak barrels. In addition to the money
it saves, new operational efficiencies can directly deliver
better product quality if you will only design them that
way.

▶ *Strive for across-the-board quality.* A pebble thrown into
the Internet pond sends ripples all around the world. If
you relax your quality standards, one or another customer

is going to alert the world online and do irreparable damage to your brand. In that way, a problem in one part of your business can taint all that you do. That's why Clos du Bois maintains high standards for all its wines. Over the years, one authority after another has commented on the across-the-board excellence of the company's line. Clos du Bois understands that consumers today are too savvy, too selective, and too tuned to the Internet, so it won't take a chance on reducing the quality of even a single product and getting zapped by the online services.

▶ *Make quality sacred.* For a company to achieve a consistently high level of quality in its actions and operations, it must embed a commitment to that goal deep within its culture. The dedication to quality must become a shared value among all employees, or that high standard cannot and will not be maintained.

Clos du Bois shows its devotion to quality in ways large and small. The physical appearance of the operation is always neat and clean. The company seeks to make its commitment to excellence visible, because in such matters actions are more important than words. Any award given one of its wines, for example, is a cause for a celebration including a glass of wine for all. Employees are pledged to creating the best wine they can and then given the authority to make it happen.

▶ *Watch your channels.* Quality sells itself, they say, but don't count on it. Good distribution channels are essential, and a weak distributor or an ignorant retailer can do your brand serious harm. So, choose your channel partners

carefully and, if necessary, educate them about your
product. That's what Clos du Bois did. After initially
putting his wine in restaurants and competitions to
establish a reputation for quality, Frank Woods carefully
selected his distributors and retailers and devoted long
hours to teaching sales reps how to sell it. He also gave
retailers shelf cards to educate potential customers about
his wine.

Today, the Internet has become the latest new channel to
market, if not for direct sales then to provide information
about the product or to build a community around it. The
challenge is to align your online presence with your other
marketing approaches and with your brand as a whole. A
multichannel strategy must be managed to keep messages
and experiences consistent so as not to put your strategy
of quality at risk.

▶ *Keep testing the limits of growth.* A former chairman
of American Express once asked me whether all great
companies must eventually fail. History suggests that they
must, that strong growth tends toward disaster: Witness
the recent woes of the auto industry. But that is not to
suggest that failure should be accepted as a given. Growth
with quality can be managed if you can determine at an
early stage where breakdowns that come with scale might
occur and adjust for them.

When I talked with Chris, he indicated that Clos du Bois was actively debating just how large any winery can grow before the quality of its operations and product starts to weaken. A shortage of grapes might become a limiting factor. This much is sure: The impressive efficiency of the company has made the challenges that come with growth far more manageable. Efficiency, combined with a focus on quality, can do that for you.

Having examined hundreds of companies in the process of writing this book and those that preceded it in the series, I know that there is no single formula for succeeding when you take on the execution of a worthwhile strategy, especially in a challenging economy. But some general principles can help guide your efforts. The only caveat is that you must adapt them to the culture of your own enterprise. Here, in brief, are the principles I hope you take away from what you've just read.

- ▶ *Be of two minds.* Executing during challenging times requires you to manage two seemingly conflicting ideas at the same time, and that can be tricky. Most companies naturally focus on costs to improve their performance, but if you merely reduce costs and head count, you run the risk of also reducing your capabilities, product quality, and service levels. To keep customers coming back during difficult times, it's just as important to deliver more value as well. Customers want to receive more value from what they buy—and lower costs. Besides, when the economy recovers, as it eventually will, you'll want to be a stronger, more capable enterprise, not a weaker one.

- ▶ *Get focused.* To survive in a challenging economy, you must look at your products and processes with an eye toward improvement. Ask yourself, "How can we increase product quality? Where in our delivery of service can we do a better job? Where are the opportunities for us

**EPILOGUE**

to leapfrog competitors with radically new products and services?" Look broadly across your market, not just at poor-performing segments because high profits often hide gross inefficiencies. Figure out where costs are concentrated, and zero in on reducing them while dramatically improving performance.

▶ *Look outside your walls.* Many companies have a tendency to look inward when the going gets rough. But developing a bunker-like mentality can keep you from seeing opportunities in the wider world. For instance, you might acquire your way to capabilities that can ratchet up your competitiveness capabilities that might otherwise take years to develop. Bargains abound in tough times, so be on the lookout for corporate combinations that can add value to your product or service and bring efficiencies to how you operate.

Working more closely with your suppliers and the companies that distribute or sell your products can provide other, often-overlooked opportunities. Look for ways to improve processes across your industry's entire value chain.

▶ *Set targets with greatness in mind.* You can't improve your business unless you know where to add value and where to improve efficiency. Be disciplined about setting targets, specifying the whats and the whens, and how progress will be measured and at what intervals. But don't be afraid to elevate your ambitions and aspirations wherever you can. As you read in Chapter 3, "Radically Restructuring to Deliver," there is nothing like an inspiring objective to rally an organization.

Reporting on your initiative calls for a sensitive touch; too frequent reports distract people from their work, and too few risk surprises that can slow or even derail the plan. You can get a sense for proper reporting schedules when you map out your desired improvements.

▶ *Balance consolidation with localization.* Efficiency programs often focus on combining like functions, departments, and processes. But be careful not to go too far. Some processes are best handled at a local level, close to the customer. Determining which processes should be centralized and which should be kept local is another example of having to think with two minds.

▶ *Integrate and collaborate.* When too many departments and too many functions are involved in doing the work, efficiency is lost as the work moves through the organization. Only fundamental redesign can bring about substantial efficiencies, and various programmatic approaches, such as quality programs, lean manufacturing, and reengineering, are highlighted in this book. Select the one that best fits your needs and culture. But if you can't make structural changes in how your company does its work, at least force collaboration across departments, functions, and business units.

▶ *Pay attention to the soft side.* Nothing changes inside an enterprise unless people, skills, and behaviors change. You can redesign strategies, processes, systems, and structures, but you can't deliver without extraordinary effort and dedication from your people. By attending to the so-called soft side, you can soon find that the hard work of delivering is being done according to plan.

▶ *Use efficiency to leverage quality.* It is almost counterintuitive to consider that improved product quality can be driven by greater efficiency. Being more efficient allows you to put more resources into quality, of course, but the surprise comes when you realize that efficient processes lead directly to a higher-quality product or service. Efficiency and quality are complementary, not contradictory.

▶ *Know what's going on from top to bottom.* Executives and senior managers often create too much distance between themselves and operations. A successfully executed strategy demands that you pay great attention not only to what's going on inside your company's operations, but also inside those of your suppliers and distributors. All the executives and managers featured in this book have a keen sense of what's going on in their enterprises, intervening when necessary with timely action. You can't make intelligent decisions unless you know what's going on.

▶ *Don't put off until tomorrow what needs doing today.* A business that's in trouble, whether it's because of the economy or a hard-charging competitor, needs help immediately. The longer you wait, the bigger the challenge. Hope may spring eternal, but business problems generally don't get better on their own. Inaction just makes things worse. The sooner you act, the easier the job will be—though it will never be that easy.

▶ *Don't let plans and budgets deter action.* I believe in the discipline of plans and budgets, but, sometimes, large organizations use them as an excuse for inaction. "We don't have the money for that this year," they'll say, or "It's not in the plan." Today's economy demands action, a willingness to find resources to get things done. It may mean stopping other work, transferring resources from one area to another. Hard decisions, to be sure, but nothing can change otherwise.

## "The sun will come up tomorrow, and the bridges will continue to bear traffic."

Remembering all these principles may be difficult when you are engaged in the gritty work of executing during challenging times. So, I want to recall a quote that I cited in the first book in this series, *Outsmart!*. When the economist Paul Samuelson was once asked what would happen if a great monetary crisis, then looming, actually happened, he replied, "The sun will come up tomorrow, and the bridges will continue to bear traffic." Whatever happens, the world will keep turning, markets will come back, and opportunities will abound. The challenge will be in how you execute to take advantage of these opportunities. I hope that you have been inspired, as I have been, by the businesses in this book that deliver each and every day.

**FINANCIAL TIMES**

In an increasingly competitive world, it is quality
of thinking that gives an edge—an idea that opens new
doors, a technique that solves a problem, or an insight
that simply helps make sense of it all.

We work with leading authors in the various arenas
of business and finance to bring cutting-edge thinking
and best-learning practices to a global market.

It is our goal to create world-class print publications
and electronic products that give readers
knowledge and understanding that can then be
applied, whether studying or at work.

To find out more about our business
products, you can visit us at www.ftpress.com.

Made in the USA
Lexington, KY
07 October 2011